"*The Land Is Not Empty* is a tremendous, liberating work full of love for God and neighbor. Whether you are unfamiliar with the Doctrine of Discovery or are a lifelong Christocentric promoter of Indigenous rights, this book is for you."

—**NATHAN CARTAGENA**, race scholar and assistant professor of philosophy at Wheaton College

"Sarah Augustine's message is an urgent call to action: abolish the Christian Doctrine of Discovery. The legacies of colonial conquest scaffold our present world of inequality and climate change. Abolishing the Doctrine means more than repudiation of church dogma codified in law and social norms justifying dispossession, genocide, and exploitation. It means restoration and repairing wrongs done to Indigenous people. The Doctrine is a 'structural sin,' Augustine writes, and it requires collective action on the part of the faith community. Justice begins by hearing her call to action—a prophecy of a better world."

—**NICK ESTES** (Lakota), author of *Our History Is the Future: Standing Rock versus the Dakota Access Pipeline, and the Long Tradition of Indigenous Resistance*

"With an interplay of history, Bible, testimony, analysis, and intimate personal narrative, Sarah Augustine paints a devastating picture of the Doctrine of Discovery as structural sin. Proclaiming a vision of right relationship with Indigenous peoples around the globe, she compels a radical new theological imagination and bold acts of justice from those who aspire to live the mandate of Jesus."

—**JENNIFER HENRY**, activist theologian

"If insight is the prophetic task—and I believe it is—this book is prophecy. Beautifully weaving together her moving personal narrative, the narrative of destructive colonization, the narrative of courageous resistance and life of Indigenous Peoples around the world, and, through it all, the narrative of resurrection and Jesus' promise of the world to come, Sarah Augustine engages your mind, your heart, and your future."

—**THE MOST REV. MARK MACDONALD**, National Indigenous Anglican Archbishop of the Anglican Church of Canada

THE LAND IS NOT EMPTY

FOLLOWING JESUS IN DISMANTLING THE DOCTRINE OF DISCOVERY

SARAH AUGUSTINE

HERALD PRESS

Harrisonburg, Virginia

Herald Press
PO Box 866, Harrisonburg, Virginia 22803
www.HeraldPress.com

Study guides are available for many Herald Press titles at www.HeraldPress.com.

THE LAND IS NOT EMPTY
© 2021 by Herald Press, Harrisonburg, Virginia 22803. 800-245-7894.
   All rights reserved.
Library of Congress Control Number: 2021933134
International Standard Book Number: 978-1-5138-0829-1 (paperback);
   978-1-5138-0831-4 (ebook)
Printed in United States of America
Cover and interior design by Merrill Miller
Cover art: *East of Cassoday* by Robert Regier

Portions of this book have appeared in the following publications and have been adapted here with permission:

Mennonite Church USA five-part blog series on the Doctrine of Discovery, February–July 2015. "The Doctrine of Discovery and the Anabaptist Coalition to Dismantle It" in *Resistance: Addressing Violence in a Peace Church*, ed. Cameron Altaras and Carol Penner (Elkhart, IN: Institute of Mennonite Studies, forthcoming). "What Would Justice Look Like?," *Intersections: MCC Theory and Practice Quarterly* 6, no. 1 (Winter 2018): 2–4. "Right Relationship Means Giving Up Power," *The Mennonite*, April 1, 2019. Dismantling the Doctrine of Discovery Coalition, reparations resource *Reparations and Private Property*.

The names and identifying details of many of the people who appear in these pages have been changed to protect their privacy. I have chosen to change the names and details of vulnerable people to ensure they will not face criticism or threat for the inclusion of their stories.

25 24 23   10 9 8 7 6 5 4

For the ones who will come after us

Contents

Foreword

IT WAS A cool Sunday morning in late winter/early spring. We had been receiving an unusual number of steady storms, some rain and some snow, for over a week. We had been stuck in our hogan for the duration, and our supply of food and water was beginning to run low. The situation was not yet dire, but our concern was high enough that we had begun melting snow to conserve our precious remaining supply of drinking water.

My family and I had moved to this area on the Navajo Nation less than two years earlier from Denver, Colorado, where I had pastored a church called the Christian Indian Center. On the reservation we lived in a small one-room hogan on a sheep camp that did not have running water or electricity and was accessible only by dirt road.

Because the road was not paved, even a small amount of moisture could make it impassable. The ground was clay, so when it got wet the road became like an oil slick. During the winter snows our road was drivable mostly at night after the mud had frozen solid. But spring snowfalls were challenging, as it rarely got cold enough to freeze the mud solid. Meaning the best option was to wait for dry weather to return.

A couple of days prior, we found the ground had frozen a little more overnight. We and our neighbors hastily piled into our car and attempted to drive out. But in less than two miles, we realized we were not going to make it, as we were sinking into the ruts of the road created by others in the area who had attempted the same feat. We got stuck in one particularly muddy spot and had to abandon our car there, all of us walking back home.

And so, on that Sunday morning, our concern was growing. Our food and water supplies were running low, and because of the forecast we did not expect to get out for several more days. We intended to meet with two of our neighbors who were also Christians to pray and study the Bible. We had done this several times prior, but that Sunday felt different—a little more desperate.

We had a third neighbor who did not normally join us for church, but when we sat down I asked if anyone knew where he was. His sister replied, "He left a few minutes ago. He is walking to the road to meet some people and get us some groceries." I was immediately humbled. The paved road was over six miles away. It would take him hours to walk there through the mud and then even longer to return, carrying heavy groceries. At that moment, I knew what I had to do. I excused myself, slipped on some shoes, grabbed a jacket, and ran out the door looking for my neighbor. I had prepared to teach that morning about the love of God, while he was very practically demonstrating the love of God by walking to the road to pick up groceries.

I caught up with him a few hundred yards from the house and walked with him the remainder of the way. When we arrived at the road some other family members were waiting for us with groceries and jugs of water. We loaded up our backpacks, grabbed bags of groceries, and began the long six-mile hike back home.

I will never forget that day. My neighbor was a quiet man, a boarding school survivor who had lived in that area of the reservation most of his life. He herded sheep and mostly kept to himself, and I was never quite sure of the best way to get to know him. But that walk changed everything—he talked freely. It seemed as if every tree, every path had a different story. Down one path was where his sister and brother-in-law had gotten stuck in the mud on their wedding night. Another tree was where his mother had given birth to him. A third area was where he had seen other people get stuck. Every mile we walked was filled with stories, often told with a smile, and many ending in laughter.

In fact, I became one of those funny stories myself. In my haste to get out the door, I did not take time to put on boots but instead slipped on some light sneakers. The longer we walked and the warmer it got, the muddier that path became. When we finally arrived at the paved road, my sneakers and my feet were caked in mud! Everyone laughed with me at my poor choice of shoes. But before we headed home, one of the relatives offered their brand-new boots to me in exchange for my sneakers. It was hardly a fair trade, but it was blatantly obvious that my sneakers were never going to get me home. I humbly accepted.

That day was a turning point, not only in my relationship with our neighbor but in our sense of belonging in that community. No longer were we outsiders hearing stories about how hard life on the reservation was. That walk was a milestone in our journey to becoming insiders, people with shared stories, hard stories, but many told with a smile and often ending in laughter.

In the first chapter of this book, Sarah Augustine will masterfully draw you into her story by talking about the difference in perspective that people have depending on the mode of transportation they take. She will tell you about the difference between driving through her neighborhood and walking through it. She will talk about her connection with the Indigenous People of Suriname and the difference between taking a short trip to their remote lands by airplane and traveling there over several days by canoe. Through personal stories, interpretations of Scriptures, and references to historical documents and events, she will talk about her journey to learn about, understand, and confront the Doctrine of Discovery.

The journey she describes in this book is beautiful, and at times it is uncomfortable, difficult, and overwhelming. No one can ever be fully prepared for this journey, and if you knew everything the journey might entail you would probably never go. Sarah is walking through the mud in an attempt to get all of us some much-needed supplies. Meanwhile, many in the family of God are sitting comfortably in our churches. I invite you to read this book and allow Sarah to help you step out of your comfort zone so that after you are finished reading you might grab a jacket, hastily put on some sneakers, and take a walk with someone who is already on the journey.

—Mark Charles, coauthor of *Unsettling Truths: The Ongoing, Dehumanizing Legacy of the Doctrine of Discovery*

Contributor's Preface

I FIRST HEARD THE WORDS "Doctrine of Discovery" in 2013, on a bus coming back from a tour of the U.S.-Mexican border with my friend and pastoral colleague Weldon. He and I had worked together on LGBTQ and other justice issues in Mennonite Church USA for years. The tour exposed us to the immense difficulties and injustices faced by immigrants crossing through the Sonoran Desert en route to low-wage jobs in the United States.

"The Doctrine of Discovery is the basis for so much of the oppression we're fighting against in the U.S. and worldwide," he said animatedly. "You really must meet Sarah Augustine and hear her talk about this." Sarah, he explained, was a member of his church who worked with Indigenous People around the world who were being harmed by neocolonization.

I trusted Weldon . . . but I was also skeptical. I struggled to understand how a five-hundred-year-old church doctrine mattered today. It seemed abstract, even esoteric. Little did I know that I would help found the Dismantling the Doctrine of Discovery Coalition a year later with Sarah and Anita Amstutz, another friend and pastoral colleague. The Spirit moves in mysterious and powerful ways, I found, especially when your life begins intersecting with Sarah's.

Since 2014, I have talked on the phone with Sarah nearly every Friday morning for an hour or more. Through these conversations, I learned just how relevant and present the Doctrine of Discovery really is. This wasn't because Sarah, in some kind of professorial way, talked me through a linear exposition of the Doctrine of Discovery, starting with the fourteenth century and moving sequentially into the present. Our conversations were more a spiraling unfolding of stories and scholarship that, over the course of years, has changed the way I view the world. These conversations enabled me to see the world, I believe, as it really is. They enabled me to see the deep structures of colonization that are so invisible to people like myself, a white, middle-class person.

I learned that the Doctrine of Discovery was a five-hundred-year-old heresy that justified both the seizure of lands from Indigenous People, their enslavement and domination, and the Portuguese slave trade from West Africa (the latter is often not as well known). I learned that these doctrines came to constitute a legal and philosophical framework of domination that—far from being a historical relic—structures our world into the present. There are Indigenous Peoples right now in Suriname, whom you will read about in this book, who are losing their ancestral homelands to U.S. and Canadian mining corporations because they don't legally own these homelands. They don't own these homelands because the Doctrine of Discovery made it permissible—even moral!—for European discoverers to lay legal claim to lands inhabited by non-Christians. In the United States, this framework was enshrined into law in a landmark 1823 Supreme Court case and was cited as recently as 2005 in another Supreme Court ruling.

I began to see how this church doctrine, which had become encoded into law, policy, and worldview, was *the* engine of domination, just as Weldon had said. I felt I was facing head on the powers and principalities and the spiritual forces of evil spoken of in Ephesians 6:12.

And this wasn't an abstract evil. This was an evil in which my family had actively participated. The Hochstetlers arrived in Pennsylvania in the 1700s and settled on land bought from the Leni Lenape (Delaware) people by William Penn. I'd known about this for decades. But it was only as I was learning about the Doctrine of Discovery that I realized my Amish ancestors were the first Europeans to settle the part of Ohio where I grew up, on land that had been "cleared" of its Native inhabitants only several years before. My pacifist ancestors got their land as a result of military conquest.

My conversations with Sarah have changed my life—and continue to do so. One of the reasons I'm so excited about this book is because it gives you the experience I had talking with Sarah over the years. It is not a linear, didactic exposition on the Doctrine of Discovery but the same spiraling unfolding of story and scholarship I experienced. By the end of this book, I predict you, too, will not see the world the same way you did at the beginning of it. Be prepared to be changed.

And be prepared to be challenged. Sarah possesses one of the strongest and most faithful prophetic voices I know. When she speaks, I hear the voice of the Hebrew prophets and of Jesus. It's a prophetic voice that often speaks in dualisms—the forces of death versus the forces of life—that help us cut through the complexities that can obscure reality and see what is really at stake. This prophetic voice may sometimes sound harsh or "one-sided" to you. You may find yourself saying, "But what about X? Or what about Y?" You may find yourself wanting to complexify or nuance some of what Sarah says, to tone it down.

I want to challenge folks—especially those who are white settlers like myself—to bracket that response for a while and really listen to Sarah's voice. Allow yourself to take it in before you resist its full force. Sarah is giving you a great gift: her own hard-won moral clarity. She is more than capable of complex, nuanced thought, as you will also realize reading this book. Had she not committed herself to activism on behalf of the world's most vulnerable people, she could easily be a PhD teaching sociology at a university. I rely on Sarah's scholarly analysis to help me understand the world. But I rely on her prophetic voice to help me understand how to be a faithful follower of Jesus.

In fact, it is Sarah's deep connection to Jesus and the Spirit of Life that has most changed my life. Sarah has staked her life in the trust that the "sacred forms of life, known in Jewish, Christian and Muslim traditions as God, is coursing through all of creation, and is bringing about healing and liberation despite all evidence to the contrary."[1] Because of this deep trust, I have never seen her give in to despair or fear or give up, even though she has been fighting human rights abuses her entire life. On one of our calls, she said to me, "There is this agenda of creation that began at the beginning of time and that is ongoing. I want to be a part of that. I'm going to align myself with that. I'm going to cooperate and coordinate with the forces of life. The death-dealing forces that have been put into motion may not be able to be interrupted at this time, but I'm going to continue to live in hope for the eventual victory of creation. The only outcome of the forces of death is death. There is no victory for that side. Creation is going to go on one way or another, with us or without us. I want to collaborate with the Creator. That's what I can focus on."

In another conversation, Sarah told me that time is not linear in the Indigenous worldview; it doesn't move forward toward greater and greater progress, as it does in the Western worldview. The Indigenous view of time, rather, is cyclical. The point of human life is not to build monuments or further progress toward some goal. Rather, the point of human life is preservation—to preserve the creation given to us by the Creator and, when necessary, to heal and repair what has been thrown out of its natural balance.

In this worldview, the idea of individual will, Sarah told me, is silly, even a little embarrassing. What does it mean for a leaf to assert its will? Does it mean that it decides to fall to the right and not the left? There is only one will, and that is God's will, the Creator's will, she said. There is only one way, and that is the way of Life. That's what our human life is for: to be a part of the process of Life; to preserve and protect and hand down, unharmed, this Life to our children and the unborn generations; to participate in Life such that it goes onward. And if we are walking in that way of Life, she told me, then the Spirit of Life, the Creator, will be with us. We will be walking the good way.

I believe reading this book will help us all more faithfully walk the good way. It will help bring about healing and liberation. And I believe the Spirit of Life will be with you as you read it. May that be so.

—*Sheri Hostetler, pastor, poet, activist*

Introduction

THE UNITED STATES was founded on ill-gotten gains. And it has prospered.

Indigenous Peoples have been systematically disenfranchised and dispossessed as a matter of church policy for 500 years; by United States policy for 240 years.

Many historians and theologians place the Doctrine of Discovery squarely in the past. I will explain its ongoing magnitude as the primary framework that continues to define life for Indigenous Peoples around the globe.

I learned about this fact in relationship with small Indigenous and tribal communities in Suriname, in a region of South America known as the Guiana Shield. I learned about the Doctrine of Discovery by association with Peoples who are under attack, struggling for survival. The reality they face today—displacement, forced removal, dispossession, systemic discrimination—is the history of my family. I learned to understand my own history in partnership with them.

Before working in Suriname, I believed the abuse and neglect I experienced in my childhood were private matters, that the poverty and isolation I grew up with were willfully wrought by two dysfunctional people, my parents. I learned in relationship with Indigenous communities a continent away that my private situation was planned, my sense of worthlessness and hopelessness was intended by the most powerful nation on earth. My history, my present, and the future of Indigenous Peoples around the world today are all predetermined by a body of policy called the Doctrine of Discovery.

The foundational documents of the Doctrine of Discovery are a series of papal bulls, or legal decrees, created by the Christian church that explain why Europeans alone deserve to own land in what was termed the New World, and why those of European descent are deemed human while those indigenous to the land, my ancestors included, are not. Law upon law, termed precedents in the U.S. legal system, has been based on these original assumptions that continue to shape reality for Indigenous Peoples in North America and around the world today.

The evidence of this is clear. In the United States, Indigenous Peoples, when compared to other racial groups, are incarcerated at higher rates;[1] suffer from the highest rates of suicide;[2] are the least likely to graduate from high school;[3] are the most likely to live in poverty;[4] suffer disproportionately high rates of maternal and infant mortality;[5] and lag behind in home ownership, all as a result of United States policy.

In this book I speak about economic development and global economic systems, political structures of global governance (termed supranational structures), and even theology. I speak about each of these from my own viewpoint, as a simple brown woman.

I acknowledge that it is difficult to speak about economic systems when I am clearly not an economist; systems of governance when I am not a political scientist; and Scripture when I am not a seminary-trained theologian. Yet I have been called to this work, and so I speak what I have seen with my own eyes, heard with my own ears.

I speak as an internally displaced person. This book is in part a story of how I became displaced. Because my father was removed from his mother and his people as an infant, I grew up in poverty, ignorant of my own background, language, and culture. I find that I am often asked to explain myself. Who am I? Where am I from? I have been a source of curiosity and scorn for some, curiosity and exoticism for others. I am a Native woman, but I can't enroll my son in our tribe because of a legacy of trauma.

In many ways, the pattern of displacement has defined my experience living in the United States. To illustrate this tension, I offer the following story. As a young woman in college, I earned a human rights prize from the United Nations Association of New Mexico for organizing statewide support for prisoners of conscience in the early 1990s. At the event, held in a hotel ballroom, I was asked to provide the keynote address. I arrived an hour early, hoping to meet with the organizer of the event, nervous I might not know where to stand or when to speak. I entered the auditorium-sized room and sat in a chair at the back, waiting, as guests began to trickle in. When the organizer arrived, she walked directly to my chair, wearing a countenance of tense displeasure.

"Why are you sitting there?" she barked at me. "Serve the drinks to guests as they come in! Catering staff ought not be sitting at all." I was stunned and embarrassed. I apologized and served the drinks. While my documented race and status may be ambiguous, my status in society has not been.

As I have traveled far and wide seeking help on behalf of Indigenous Peoples, I have had the privilege of visiting with Christians from many denominations, including denominational executives and decision-makers, CFOs, mission boards, and community leaders. Much of what I share in this text refers to my personal experience petitioning church institutions.

I have also visited with congregations across the United States and in parts of Europe. Many Christians have voiced a reluctance to get involved because they do not feel qualified. Well, neither am I "qualified." There are surely many people better formally prepared than me; but since an elder in Suriname asked for my help, and I said yes, I have been sent into places I never imagined I could go. What I have learned is that there is no qualification for resisting oppression. Anyone can resist oppression. We must all resist oppression.

My heart is for peace and reconciliation. Truths I hold as self-evident may be at odds with truths you may hold sacred. But I long for conciliation, for repair. I tell my son that he is a miracle—every Native child born is a miracle. We exist despite massive efforts to extinguish our existence. But I have no patience for animosity or bitterness. For the survival of my people, and for all people, we must mutually seek repair.

This book is an attempt to share what I have seen and experienced with my own eyes. I share it because I believe it's wrong not to. The people with whom I have partnered, people who don't have a voice, must have their petitions held up. So that's what I am doing.

Some opinion leaders I respect have disagreed with my views about the Scripture: about what constitutes the good news and my reaction to the stories that have justified manifest destiny. But the views I express here speak to the people and Peoples who have experienced the world as I do, and Christianity as I have. Whatever the theories that justify the rightness of the dominant narrative that Christianity has espoused, its impact on my life and the lives of Indigenous Peoples around the globe is irrefutable.

The systems of economics and governance, principalities and powers, are subtle and do much of their business in the dark. While I have tried diligently to describe what I have seen and experienced of them, I recognize that even after years of study and persistent petitions, what I know is a tiny fraction of all that goes on. I sincerely hope that those of you who come after me will take up the work of learning them, pursuing them, in the cause of justice—living out the good news—justice for the oppressed.

ONE

The Doctrine of Discovery and Me

I LIVE AMONG THE YAKAMA PEOPLE in central Washington State, specifically on a small ranch just below the precise place where the sky touches the earth: Toppenish Ridge. The place where I stay is nestled against a series of curved foothills, along the southern edge of the earthen bowl surrounding the Yakima Valley.[1]

I am blessed to be welcomed as a neighbor among the Yakama people because in a nation that equates freedom with the open road, gasoline, and automobiles, I'm a walker. Cars have always made me nervous; I was an adult before I took my first driving test and earned a license. Although I have a car, I have owned one for just half my adult life. This "walking" sensibility is a gift where I live. It allows me to see fully the world and community around me.

Although I live in a rural community where small towns are dozens of miles apart, it is a walking place to many people, especially among the Yakama peoples. You may notice if you visit this place that Yakama people pop up in unexpected places. Seemingly empty lots. Medians. The "blank" spaces between buildings.

When driving-culture people look at an unfamiliar place, they look to roads. Homes, neighborhoods, businesses, even landmarks like mountains and rivers are viewed in relation to roads. Maps define communities by the roads that snake through them, guide travelers from where they are to where they wish to go.

If a person is looking at a place through the frame of roads, roadless places are not visible. This is why a road-centric person who is pumping gas at the Yakamart gas station may be startled when a local person is suddenly standing nearby. Where did this person come from? The road-centric person looks to the left and the right. No car drove in. Did this person materialize out of the weeds? Actually, the person was rendered invisible by simply inhabiting the space that is irrelevant when traveling by road.

As a walking person, I am open to thinking about space in shorter distances, since I walk to familiar places accessible easily on foot. Whether in Manhattan or on the reservation, distance and time take on different meanings without a car. When I walk the three miles of Island Road from the main road to my house, the farms along the fence do not seem small or uniform at all, as they might to someone whizzing by in a car. If you walked with me, the burning sensation in your calves would force you to notice the hill we would crest, the place where the pavement peters out into gravel. You would see the clear distinction between the overgrazed pastureland on the east side of the road and the wildlife preserve to the west. You would notice the difference between a field worked with large equipment (tilled into neat rows) and pastures meant for livestock (plenty of weeds). You would appreciate the different foliage on the hills (green orchard grass or brown wheatgrass) and in the hollows (riparian toolies and cattails).

If you imagine space through a walking perspective, what may appear to be an "empty lot" from a car window becomes a rich ecosystem. What seemed to be a strip of land between buildings is actually a wide thoroughfare. From the walking perspective, any land good for foot travel is a safe distance from the dusty, reckless roads.

As a walker, as one who dwells on a reservation that is ill-defined by the dominant culture, the world between the spaces where most people travel is where I live: off the map.

Now imagine with me traveling to the Wayana people in Suriname, located on the northeastern Atlantic coast of South America. To get there requires a series of international flights, either through Europe or the Caribbean. Once in the capital, Paramaribo, one must either charter a bush airplane or travel on the Tapanahony River for three days through dense rainforest to get to the village of Apetina. Imagine the difference between flying over the dense canopy for two hours and traveling by canoe for three days, sleeping in the rainforest for three nights. The difference in the experience of the distance traveled is astonishing.

In Suriname, the national government claims that the rainforest that makes up most of the country is predominantly uninhabited. From the vantage of an airplane speeding high above dense rainforest canopy, it certainly seems to be. But traveling the slow way, the way of the Wayana, you may see things differently.

Indigenous Peoples persist in traditional cultivation, hunting, and gathering cycles to provide the food, building materials, and medicines to support their population. Originally, low-population-density tribes in this rainforest planted gardens and hunted in large areas on a cycle that could span decades.[2] This ensured that the poor rainforest soil would replenish itself after light cultivation.

In the 1980s, Christian missionaries in Suriname began the process of consolidating the twelve distinct tribes of Indigenous Peoples into village clusters.[3] Village clusters were established to efficiently proselytize communities (from the missionary viewpoint), and to remove inhabitants from potentially resource-rich regions (from the government viewpoint). Once mission villages were established, the Suriname government declared the interior "empty" and therefore open for resource exploration and extraction.

The Suriname government does not take an actual census of the rainforest population. The official numbers reported, an estimated 4 percent of the national population, are based on the imposed "village" population estimates only. Meanwhile, according to the government, the interior lands are "uninhabited" by humans.

Terra nullius

Suriname's policy toward Indigenous Peoples did not originate in this small region. It is based on the principles defined by *terra nullius*, a Latin phrase meaning "empty land," a theological and legal doctrine that gave land title to Christian European states who would assume sovereignty over "discovered lands." Under *terra nullius*, "discovered" lands were considered devoid of human beings if the original people who had lived there—defined as "heathens, pagans, and infidels"—were not ruled by a "Christian prince." The *terra nullius* doctrine became the cornerstone of the Doctrine of Discovery.

The "Doctrine of Discovery" does not refer to just one church doctrine, nor are its impacts confined to theological issues. The Doctrine of Discovery is a theological, philosophical, and legal framework dating to the fifteenth century that gave Christian governments moral and legal right to invade and seize Indigenous lands and dominate Indigenous Peoples. This pattern of oppression began with papal bulls, or decrees. One of the most infamous is *Romanus Pontifex*, issued by Pope Nicholas V in 1455. This bull granted the Portuguese king the right to "invade, search out, capture, vanquish, and subdue all Saracens [Muslims] and pagans whatsoever, and other enemies of Christ wheresoever placed," and to "reduce their persons to perpetual slavery" and to "apply and appropriate to himself and his successors" all of these peoples' sovereign lands, possessions, and goods.[4] In other words, *Romanus Pontifex* justified enslaving and seizing the land and possessions of anyone who was not a Christian, setting the stage for colonization as well as the enslavement of African people by Europeans. Christopher Columbus, under the direction of the Spanish Crown, was similarly instructed to "discover and conquer," "subdue," and "acquire" distant lands, and John Cabot was given similar direction by the British Crown. North and South America were colonized according to this pattern, as were Australia and New Zealand.

The Doctrine of Discovery may sound like something from the past, a discrete historical event from back when Christians didn't "know better." Unfortunately, nothing could be further from the truth. The Doctrine of Discovery formed the deep structure of colonization that continues to oppress Indigenous

Peoples and dispossess them of their land today. Papal decrees had the force of law in a time when there was no such thing as the separation of church and state. Over time, these decrees dictating who was able to own land in colonized countries became the basis of international law, and most Western countries incorporated this international law into their national laws and policies as well.

For instance, in the United States, the Christian Doctrine of Discovery was adopted into U.S. law by the Supreme Court in the celebrated case *Johnson v. M'Intosh* in 1823. Writing for a unanimous court, Chief Justice John Marshall said that Christian European nations had assumed "ultimate dominion" over the lands of America during the Age of Discovery and that upon "discovery," the Indigenous People had lost "their rights to complete sovereignty, as independent nations" and retained only a right of "occupancy" in their lands. According to Marshall, the United States, upon winning its independence in 1776, became a successor nation to the right of "discovery" and acquired the power of "dominion" from Great Britain. As late as 2005, Ruth Bader Ginsburg cited the landmark 1823 decision in *City of Sherrill v. Oneida Indian Nation of New York*. The ruling held that the repurchase of tribal lands did not restore tribal sovereignty.

We can see the Doctrine of Discovery manifest in Arizona today, where the San Carlos Apache are battling to protect a sacred site called Oak Flat (Chi'chil Bildagoteel). Because of the Doctrine of Discovery, the San Carlos Apache do not legally own this place of ceremony and prayer near Phoenix that they have visited from time immemorial. Instead, the land is owned by the U.S. Forest Service. As of this writing, the U.S. Congress plans to transfer this land to an Australian copper mining company in the first quarter of 2021. Mining will desecrate this sacred site. This is but one of thousands of examples of how the Doctrine of Discovery operates today. All around the world, the Doctrine of Discovery legitimates resource extraction from ancestral Indigenous lands. Mining, fracking, logging, water theft, plantation agriculture, and other extractive industries take resources from Indigenous communities to benefit those descended from Europeans and colonial or postcolonial nations. In addition, these extractive industries often pollute the lands, water, and bodies of Indigenous Peoples on Indigenous homelands without penalty or censure.

I have found that most people are amazed when they hear this. The dominant narrative in the United States explains that Indigenous Peoples either sold their lands in a fair bargain or lost their lands as a result of legal war. Regrettable, but "just how it goes." Few people have heard of the Doctrine of Discovery and are surprised when they realize that these injustices are *perfectly legal*. Because European and Western legal systems are based on precedent, the land-rights issues that Indigenous Peoples face today—reflected in legal decisions made by the U.S. Supreme Court and high courts around the globe—are a result of policy set by the church before Columbus and reinforced by legal structures for five centuries. Land and resource theft has been perfectly legal for more than five hundred years!

A paradigm of domination

However, the Doctrine of Discovery affects more than just who owns the land. It is actually a paradigm of domination that is threaded through all our societal institutions, not just in the United States but around the globe. This is because, to legitimize the taking of land, the Doctrine of Discovery had to establish the ideology that Indigenous Peoples were subhuman and fundamentally inferior to Europeans.[5] As I will discuss in more detail in chapter 6, Old Testament interpretations that justified genocide became a religious and moral framework that then shaped every human institution in the "discovered world," and its worldview was reinforced in every aspect of social life. It has been repeated and practiced by every generation to this day, evident in everything from who is incarcerated to who enters a foster home to who receives prenatal care to the way we teach American history in the public education system to Supreme Court decisions relating to land tenure.

Once the inferior status of Indigenous Peoples was defined, the second strategy was to deny our existence. Defining the status of Indigenous Peoples as inferior to Europeans was effective strategy in the early stages of land occupancy when open conflict was still commonplace. However, denial that Indigenous Peoples *exist* was a strategy created with longevity in mind. For instance, in the United States, segregating Indigenous Peoples onto "reservations" (portions of land that are often the poorest in natural resources and lacking in infrastructure) isolated the problem of "the Indian" and swept it out of the view of the dominant culture. The U.S. Allotment Act of 1887 privatized the vast majority of Native American land and broke up Indigenous collective holdings of Indigenous land. Those who belonged to tribes that were unlucky enough to be denied federal recognition were defined out of existence. Tens of thousands were forced to assimilate in large cities away from their homelands and were stripped of their identity in the collective consciousness, that is, the shared beliefs, ideas, and moral norms in popular culture.[6] What is an "Indian" off the reservation?

Those who belonged to tribes denied federal recognition were defined out of existence, since "real Indians" are issued a card and assigned a number. Outside their history, language, and relationship to a homeland, Indigenous People who have not been assigned a number are not recognized by the dominant culture. Nostalgia for "Indians" is held in the collective North American consciousness, at least for the ones who come from a bygone era defined by rebellion, horses, and Hollywood mysticism. But "real Indians," our collective mythology holds, are long gone. The assimilated Native Americans of the present day are simply in the crowd of brown faces on the margins of the mainstream, assumed to be recent immigrants from foreign shores.

I am one of those brown faces, which is all I can ever claim to be. Like many Indigenous People who dwell in North America, I am the product of a diaspora: the history, language, tradition, and genetics of my people were wrenched from a place and thrown to the wind, divided for all time. In the language of the arrow of time, where progress moves in one direction, I am an assimilated person.

My lineage is similar to Indigenous People throughout the Americas. My mother's people are originally from southern Colorado, a people twice colonized: first by the Spanish, then by the northern Europeans. Although not one of her relatives can be traced to a border crossing, her childhood was marked by white locals telling her to "go back to Mexico." My father was raised in a Catholic boys' home. Segregated orphanages like the Catholic charity where he grew up were common in the 1940s, as was the practice of removing Native Americans from their homes and relocating them to cities. Both of my parents grew up on the margins of society, neither with parents. When I asked my mother where I came from, she would say, "The Planet Earth. Your father and I are like Adam and Eve."

No history. No extended family. No identity.

This process of un-naming, of depatriating, of denying, is ongoing in Suriname. As the rainforest is eradicated by deforestation, hydropower generation, and mineral extraction, thousands of Indigenous and tribal people are streaming to the capital city. Their government denies their existence as a matter of policy. The government does not include rainforest peoples in a census that has never contained a category for Indigenous Peoples. Their ancestral lands are declared "empty" and thus available for the taking. Global corporations are free to exploit the resources of the interior region of Suriname, presumed empty, with the collaboration of the Suriname government. International institutions agree that the rainforest peoples in Suriname will be lucky to survive another generation.[7] Those "lucky" enough to survive starvation, displacement, and disease caused by contaminated food and water will become like me: identityless.

A divine call to an "empty" land

Many people that I meet have never heard of Suriname. They don't actually know which continent it is on. How did I end up in Suriname, a land so far from my own?

A friend of mine from church (a man who ultimately became my husband), Dan Peplow, served in Suriname as environmental advisor to the American Embassy in the capital of Paramaribo. He was involved with a study the embassy had commissioned to estimate the risk of mercury toxicity among a village cluster in the Greenstone Belt region, an interior rainforest region rich in gold and biodiversity, and inhabited by a variety of Indigenous and tribal communities. Mercury is used in alluvial gold mining, a process that removes gold from sediments in and near rivers and streams. The Wayana, like most of the Indigenous Peoples of Suriname, live in villages along rivers that are their lifeblood and food source. Through eating fish, which is their primary source of protein, they ingest mercury, a known neurotoxin. Mercury in the food web causes stillbirths, profound birth defects, neurological damage in developing fetuses and children, damage to all parts of the nervous system in adults, disability, and premature deaths.

As part of this study, Dan was collecting hair samples from the Wayana for mercury analysis. He invited me to come and contribute a sociological perspective to the study; I was in my fifth year of a PhD program in sociology at the time. That is how I arrived on a research team investigating the impact of mercury on the bodies of Indigenous People living in the interior rainforest region of a country I had never heard of.

We traveled by car and then by boat to get to the community of what looked to me like shacks covered by thatched roofs arranged around a central meeting area. My task was to monitor the conversation, take notes, and observe. I sat in the community square on a wood bench in the open air, shaded by thatch. With the aid of a translator, I listened for more than eight hours in heat and high humidity as community members recounted their experiences. Dina, an elder, recounted how her home and small garden had been bulldozed while she was in the capital city receiving treatment for diabetes. When she returned to her home, a fence had been erected around the land where she had lived with her neighbors. The village land had been granted as a concession to a business interest that planned to build an eco-resort where the village had stood. The whole community now lived in a cramped, makeshift camp next to the fence.

I was with a team of a half dozen people from the United States. But Dina spoke directly to me, looking into my eyes the entire time. As she told her story, she stood up with dignity, straight-backed, despite her age and illness, and pointed her finger at me.

"This is what I want to know," she said to me, stepping toward me. "Are you going to fight with me?"

Didn't she know I was a social scientist, a volunteer? My commitment to the project was to write a report on ethics or, at the most, to find the appropriate NGO that could assist these people. And anyway, this concession for an eco-resort was outside the scope of the mining project Dan had invited me to take part in, and was considered "sustainable development." What could I possibly do to right how she had been wronged? She continued to walk toward me.

"Well?" she asked. "Are you going to fight with me? Are you going to help me?" The eyes of everyone in the square, including the people on my team, were fixed on me.

What could I say?

I looked at the translator, then back at Dina. "Okay," I said. "I will try. I will do my best."

"No," Dina said to me. "Help us! Help us, or go away."

I looked at her. Then I said, "Yes. I will help you."

This decision, made in an instant, has defined my life since. As a friend told me several years later, as I scoured the Mennonite world looking for people willing to go on a human rights delegation to Suriname, Dina had spoken my commissioning. I had received a divine call from an aging Indigenous woman and would spend the next sixteen years and counting trying to respond to that call.

Dina is the reason I became involved in the work of dismantling the Doctrine of Discovery, although at the time I voiced my commitment to her I had never heard of it. It was through her plea that I began to question how her people could lose their birthright so completely. How could what had happened to her be legal? *It turns out it is perfectly legal.* Who on the world stage would help? *No one of consequence, it turned out.* What could my local community and I do to help Dina get her home back? In exploring these urgent questions, I came to the slow realization that my own life story was framed by the Doctrine of Discovery, along with the stories of Indigenous Peoples in North America and around the globe. It also frames the story of the first beneficiary, the church.

Sounding praise

When I am in trouble, I focus on one note, pull it into my mind. It pulses red—praise. praise. praise.

In the back of the taxi, racing across the pitted road weaving through the rainforest, I search for the note that is at my center: *praise.* Small but insistent.

We have been traveling for more than twenty-four hours—on a plane from Paris to Cayenne, the capital of French Guiana, followed by a predawn bus from the city to the border marked by the Maroni River, crossing its fast-moving current, a swollen Amazon tributary just after the monsoons, and finally in a taxi with a kind woman who agreed to help us get to Suriname. I do not speak the language. Against the principles of probability, I still have my backpack.

Dan and I had crossed the river in a crowded dugout canoe with an outboard motor earlier that morning. I nearly toppled the boat and the other passengers, all of them Indigenous, as I lumbered aboard in stiff American shoes, carrying my conspicuously large backpack. Passengers sat in the middle length of the canoe, single file. No life jackets. The thirty or so travelers and our possessions weighed down the canoe to water level, the impossibly strong river current spilling in, weighing us down further as we crossed. Men sitting in the back bailed brown water. A young mother sat in front of me, holding a baby girl who reached for me over her mother's shoulder. Despite my Western clothes, she recognized my face. I reached for her and she crawled ably over her mother's shoulder, settling comfortably into my lap as her mother looked into my eyes, registering the same recognition.

Once on shore, our fellow travelers disappeared into the forest. Dan and I stood at the border; the imaginary political line drawn by the river. We stood on the shoulder of a heavily pitted road, some potholes cavernous enough to drive through. I was told they were made by land mines during the civil war from 1986-1992. We now had to find our way to the city, hundreds of kilometers away, through the forest. A tribal woman who spoke French, although I do not, indicated with sign language that she would be met by a taxi. We could share her car, if we could share the cost. I nodded—it would soon be dark and the prospect of staying the night in the forest was unimaginable. Somehow, we needed to find the customs office in the forest—we had opted to enter Suriname in the *binnenland*, or interior, because Dan had been detained during our previous trip to Suriname. Our advocacy for Indigenous Peoples who are hurt by the pollution generated from mining had begun to gain attention. We were now charged with finding the border customs office to legally enter Suriname by way of French Guiana.

When he finally arrived, the taxi driver understood Sranan Tongo—the lingua franca of the region—and agreed to take us to the customs outpost. A shirtless man with a chair, a table, and a stamp reviewed our documents.

We began the drive to the capital at a hundred miles an hour in a car without seatbelts. The road is routinely patrolled by bandits because it is a road traveled by gold miners and prospectors. I hit my head on the roof again and again as we race across the pitted road. I have not eaten in twenty-four hours, have not urinated for at least twelve.

praise. praise. praise. Slowly, the note I cling to is joined by a constellation of others. Harmonizing, discordant. Each note singular and clear. Together they pulse, filling the sky in my mind as they sound together Praise. Praise. Praise. Praise. I can hold them each, and as one. And I know that whatever happens, all is and was and will be well.

Bad Indian

I am a Bad Indian. As in suspect. I'm not registered or enrolled, for one thing. This matters especially to the enrolled, as though Indigeneity must be blessed by the federal government before it counts.

I am also a bad Indian as in, I am not the Indigenous friend you are looking for. Not so good at cocktail parties. I am not witty or self-deprecating; I don't talk in metaphors or share tribal legends. I actually tend to have a one-track mind and talk obsessively about the tedious subject of justice. And Jesus. I talk about Jesus a lot when I am talking about justice.

I am an urban Indian, for another thing. I didn't grow up on a reservation. Although I grew up in New Mexico, I didn't even know that my father was a Pueblo, or Tewa, until more than a decade after I left the state. White folks weren't fooled. I was teased mercilessly on the playgrounds of my childhood for being a "wide-faced Indian." As an adult, I have been tailed in retail spaces for decades. This retail ritual has actually fallen off somewhat since my gray hair came in at about age forty. Before that, I was a prime suspect of low-tipping, shop-lifting, lease-ditching, contract-skipping in just about every context. Because of my face. The same face that caused a Wayana child to reach for me over her mother's shoulder, and her mother, smiling weakly, handed her over to me on the bumpy trip across the river that borders Suriname and French Guiana. What did my face mean to that baby girl? How could what she saw be so different from what is perceived by my own countrymen: teachers, principals, servers, store clerks, landlords, and bank managers with whom I share a country?

Bad Indian. This also means that I am not going to dish out wisdom by the spoonful, in doses that are easily digestible. I don't play the flute and I'm not going to sing a tribal hymn in my native tongue at your church on International Day of the World's Indigenous Peoples. I'm not saying don't invite me to your church—in fact, please do. I will gladly preach about the global movement to dismantle the Doctrine of Discovery, but watch out: I will ask each and every one of you for a commitment. I guess that makes me a bad Indian too—without doubt I will make you feel uncomfortable. Bad Indian means I want justice for Indigenous Peoples everywhere, and I am pushy and difficult as I go about exploring what justice might look like and staking out a pathway for getting there.

My faith defines me. I am a Christian woman, a devoted follower of Jesus. Learning that the Christian church originated the Doctrine of Discovery sent my life spinning sideways—my understanding of the world and my place in it. How strange to find that, according to the logic of the Doctrine, I am not one of the "chosen" in the exodus story, but rather a Canaanite. Learning the precepts that underlie the Doctrine of Discovery, the ideological alibis that morally and legally justify land theft on an epic scale, shook me. Yet understanding how the Doctrine of Discovery has shaped the world, and my life in particular, has awakened in me a call to justice and peace proclaimed by Jesus in Luke 4:18-19:

> The Spirit of the Lord is upon me,
>   because the Lord has anointed me.
> He has sent me to preach good news to the poor,
>   to proclaim release to the prisoners
>   and recovery of sight to the blind,
> to liberate the oppressed,
>   and to proclaim the year of the Lord's favor.

I am awake to the reality that Jesus' call is to me, and to all creation, here and now. In unpacking and deconstructing the Doctrine of Discovery, the obligation of the church in standing with the powerless is clear. As the institution that created the moral framework for global land theft, the church has the moral obligation and the mandate to reject the Doctrine of Discovery and call systems of empire to accountability. This book seeks to share what we have learned in relationship with Indigenous Peoples, *so that the body of Christ will rise up to preach good news to the poor*, proclaim freedom for captives, sight for the blind, and liberation for the oppressed.

TWO

Laying Down Our Nets ... or How We Came to Live on a Reservation

We leave the apartment in Paramaribo at five minutes before eight in the morning and drive more than an hour to pick up two Indigenous activists, Jan and Henry. At a cultural event we had attended the evening before, Jan and Henry asked if we planned to attend the swearing-in ceremony the next morning for newly elected leadership, and if so, could we offer them a ride? Both fuel and money are scarce among community members, and large distances are difficult to navigate. We agreed to offer a ride.

We arrive at the agreed-upon meeting point at nine in the morning. They don't come out, however, until nine-thirty. At the cultural event the night before, I witnessed both of them drinking quite a bit. The ceremony is due to start at

ten in another village, and it will still take us another hour
to travel there by car. The grounds of the house where we
wait are beautiful in the morning cool—not a bad place
to wait, but Dave, our translator and guide, is irritated. He
assumes, as I do, that Jan and Henry are pretty hungover
(as is he). Once we (finally) pile into the rented truck and
begin trundling down the bauxite road, Henry asks Dan
to stop for snacks at the last store we will see for many
hours. While we buy water, Jan and Henry each get a
forty-ounce beer.

I find myself once again in a strange intersection of worlds,
forced to question my own assumptions. I feel embarrassed, waiting for Henry and Jan in the courtyard, as Dave
throws his cigarette butts on the ground. Then, as we drive,
Henry throws his beer can in the bushes on the side of
the road. This makes me uncomfortable, as it challenges my
assumptions about what it means to be Indigenous.

In the iconic public service announcement I grew up with
in the 1970s and '80s, Iron Eyes Cody canoes up a river in
an industrial area polluted with billowing clouds of aerial
emissions, then walks up the littered shore to a smoggy
freeway, where a heartless commuter tosses fast food
at his feet while Iron Eyes Cody weeps. An incredulous
voiceover explains that some people deeply respect the
natural beauty that was once the United States (apparently
Iron Eyes Cody in tribal dress), and since people started
pollution, people can stop it. My takeaway message as a
small child was that Indigenous People abhor litter. I guess
Henry didn't see that commercial, I muse to myself.

We drive to the river and cross it on a ferry. The river is beautiful—vast and silent. As we board, I can barely see the other side. I feel dislocated from time and space. The forest on all sides is implacable, a force that consumes any settlement humans throw at it. What is a beer can in the face of such momentum that a train rail is consumed a few years after it is abandoned?

———————————

As I read this journal entry nearly fourteen years after I wrote it, I am struck by the irony of my adherence to some kind of ideal:

• The rainforest should be pristine.

• The Indigenous People who live there should be noble.

• If an Indigenous person drinks too much or throws a beer can on the ground, they are discredited and unworthy of help.

• An Indigenous person who drinks too much or throws a beer can on the ground speaks for all Indigenous People in the region.

The irony is that I had the audacity to believe these things while *my* people, the people of North America, were and are actively polluting the lands, homes, and bodies of Indigenous Peoples in the Guiana Shield region, making it impossible to live there without experiencing profound health impacts. In particular, cyanide and mercury used in gold mining are poisoning Indigenous People in this eco-region that encompasses Guyana, Suriname, French Guiana, Venezuela, and parts of Brazil and Colombia.

Reading back on my words, it is clear to me that how something looked was much more important to me than what was really going on. For example, I do not mention in this journal entry that while Henry was a high chief among his people, economic development, including mining, had stripped away his access to a livelihood, so he could not even pay the three-dollar ferry to cross the river, and had to beg a ride from strangers. The delicate calculus conveyed in the journal entry simply wonders if I am somehow implicated when Henry litters by throwing a beer can in the bushes.

After returning home from our trip to Suriname when I answered Dina's call to "help us or go away," Dan and I started a nonprofit organization called Suriname Indigenous Health Fund (SIHF) to begin to address—in partnership with the Wayana and other Indigenous and tribal peoples—the health issues they were facing, to shed light on the mercury riddling our partners' communities and bodies. Dan and I knew that we did not want to "parachute" in and out of the work for justice led by the people we cared for in Suriname. The beer can incident proved a good metaphor for many potential misunderstandings that could and did occur as we as outsiders swept in and out of their lives once or twice a year.

We first offered to move to Suriname. However, community leaders urged us to stay in the United States, since pursuing human rights work in Suriname was becoming more and more difficult. Our colleagues there were getting harassed. Johan's home was raided, his computers confiscated; Erica was detained. We would be voiceless inside the country, they told us. "We need you to speak for us to the world," Karla, a close colleague and friend, insisted. "You tell us things we don't know that are happening in our own country, because you have better access to information. If you *live* here, you will face the same risk of being silenced that we do."

Still, living in our Seattle suburb far from the realities of our partners and colleagues in Suriname felt inadequate. And, after two years of working full-time on SIHF, we faced a decision point. We were both eyeing job postings in our conventional career paths. Although we had worked hard presenting our findings from Suriname around the world and had even had a hand in ensuring the United Nations Environment Programme would open an office in Suriname, there was no discernable change for the people living in affected villages. Should we move on, taking care to preserve our careers? Or should we continue to invest in what had started as a side project and had by now taken over our lives?

As we set out across the Northwest searching for a place to live that would enable us to continue our work, Dan used the language of "crossing the Rubicon." Moving meant changing our lives, probably past the point of no return. Seattle is one of the most attractive housing markets in the United States. "If you leave, you won't come back," our next-door neighbor warned us, meaning we could never buy back in once we sold our house. And if we chose to move forward with arguing for public health as a human right, it would become impossible to turn back in our careers, as well. We had already spent two years outside of roles we had anticipated; our academic credentials were collecting dust. Dan's education as a toxicologist specializing in mine-waste made job prospects working for government or industry the safest bets, but neither of these employers would be interested in hiring a PhD with documented opposition to mining interests. Meanwhile, I was veering far from a position of "scientific neutrality," a primary requirement for being taken seriously as a researcher in social science.

We realized that we were being faced with the same decision point as the disciples when Jesus asked them to follow him. "Right away," Matthew 4:20 says, "they left their nets and followed him." This was more than just stopping what they were doing to follow Jesus for a day or two. They left behind the means by which they secured their livelihood, their source of provision—their nets. Doing so was to leave behind their security to follow the call of Jesus into insecurity and uncertainty. That was the call we were also hearing.

We visited the Yakima Valley multiple times. Ultimately, we were drawn to the Yakama reservation because that is where Dan's great-grandparents had homesteaded and where his grandparents had settled. As we explored, Dan would say offhandedly, "This is where my grandfather had a blacksmith shop," and "The tent where my grandparents lived is under water now, right through there." It made sense to us that we would live in the place where Dan's ancestors had settled and that we would choose to live as neighbors, not missionaries.

And so, we chose to lay down our nets and live on the homeland of the Confederated Bands and Tribes of the Yakama Nation.

Invasion, not settlement

Velveted by the traditional shrub-steppe plants of the Yakama people, in the spring Toppenish Ridge is soft purple in the golden light of morning, deepening throughout the day from tender sage to dark green-gray by dusk, and blackening into shadow by evening. From our kitchen window, we watch it change color hour by hour, season by season. To the west of where we live stands Pahto (Mount Adams in English), the glacier-capped sacred place on this land. To the east is the Yakama Nation wildlife preserve, where ducks, geese, coyotes, blackbirds, beaver, and many other animals range freely in their natural habitat. The end of a dirt road will lead you to my home, a place rich in soil, water, and peace, a temperate oasis in the middle of what I would have called "north country" growing up in the Southwest.

I am fortunate to live in the homeland of the Yakama people, a reservation that is now a fraction of the 1,875 square miles originally guaranteed them when they ceded the bulk of their lands to the federal government in the treaty of 1855. Our ranch is 120 acres of prime agricultural land. In addition to five fine grazing pastures that we have restored to native grasses, shrubs, and habitat, it contains a small wetland fed by natural springs that is home to all manner of fish and fowl. Our home is rich in something necessary to life everywhere but especially in this dry climate that each year receives just five to seven inches of rain (enough to fill a jelly jar): water.

Like many of our neighbors, we are not tribal members of the Yakama Nation, although it is our "right" to enjoy the beauty and bounty of this place. How non-Natives came to live here requires some explanation.

When the Yakama chief Kamiakin signed the treaty in 1855 that defines life for the Yakama people to this day, it was with an understanding that the reservation would be put aside for the exclusive use of the Yakama people. But the man who brokered and signed the treaty, Isaac Stevens, governor of Washington Territory, immediately advertised to homesteaders acreage for settlement on the land.[1] He knew the treaty would not become federal law until ratified by the U.S. Congress and

President Buchanan, and this would not occur until 1859. Any homestead possessed by settlers before then would be excluded from the treaty and defended by the U.S. Army. Thus, thousands of farmers flooded to the valley that was already graded by surveyors as prime agricultural land. Among them were Dan's great-grandparents. They were simple people seeking a better life: freedom from poverty, homelessness, and religious persecution.

When Dan's kin, along with what appeared to be an invasion of settlers, took possession of Yakama lands, cattle, sheep, horses, fisheries, timber, and waterways, Kamiakin and a band of followers made a desperate attempt to defend their people in what is now called the Yakima War of 1855. This act of desperation established the Fort Simcoe garrison and the territory's justification for invoking the full force of the United States military, leading to the inevitable result: martial law.

A few miles past the town of White Swan is Fort Simcoe State Park, a bucolic family destination with acres of rolling lawns shaded by the same giant oaks that stood watch during the Yakima War. As its name implies, the park is a re-creation of the old garrison. Restored and re-created buildings provide historically accurate representations of officer quarters, soldier billets, and the general essence of military life during the time of the war, before Washington was a state. I have spent many comfortable afternoons picnicking on the spacious lawns and strolling along the trails that surround the park. It is a beautiful and interesting landmark, if a bit misleading in that it served as a military garrison for just a few years.

By 1860, the "Indian rebellion" was quelled, and the U.S. Army handed Fort Simcoe over to the Bureau of Indian Affairs (BIA), the federal agency created to be the administrator of all

Native American assets. This federal agency still exists today. The BIA was created to "civilize" Native American tribes and manage their financial affairs, and the first agent in Washington, James Wilbur, established the Yakama boarding school at Fort Simcoe.

After the defeat of the Yakama Nation, Native children of school age were forcibly removed from the custody of their parents and enrolled in this school. James Wilbur acted as administrator for over twenty years. My friend Justin recounted the horrible decision his great-grandparents and grandparents had to make: if they would not relinquish custody of their children, the BIA threatened to strip them of their land. Many Native children died in custody from diseases their immune systems had never encountered before, and many others experienced corporal punishment and forced labor. These children were punished for speaking their own language and denied the right to visit their parents.

In his dissertation "Liberating Children and Youth," John Braun uses the character of Ishmael to represent children typecast as reprobate.[2] Ishmael is the son born to Abraham by his wife's slave, Hagar. Once a legitimate son, Isaac, is born to Abraham's wife Sarah, Ishmael is sent into the desert with his mother to die. Unlike the favored son, Ishmael is cast aside without inheritance, security, or prominence. Braun points out the name Ishmael means "God hears."

As in the Abrahamic story, the Native children detained in boarding schools were made to be outcasts in their own lands, their inheritance taken away. They were typecast as sinful, illegitimate, undeserving. While God has heard their suffering, only recently are we as a society beginning to hear their stories.

At Thanksgiving the first year we lived here, Dan and I volunteered to help serve the public Thanksgiving supper at

Wilbur Memorial Church, a small Methodist congregation in White Swan. While I served turkey and mashed potatoes in the dining room, Dan spent three hours in the kitchen washing dishes. In an ironic twist, it was on Thanksgiving Day in a building named for the man who started the Native American boarding school that we met Margaret and heard her story. She and Dan stood side by side with their arms in sudsy water, both gazing out the window as she recounted her own experience at a boarding school for Native children in Oklahoma. The boarding school at Fort Simcoe had closed in 1892, thirty-two years after it opened. But federal policy favored Native student relocation to boarding schools in other states, away from what the State Department termed the "barbarous influences" of their parents. Margaret was sent to Oklahoma. She lost the knowledge of her own language forever. "It was the 1950s, and kids here still felt they had to go to boarding school to protect their parents," she said. "I still hate myself sometimes for going there. I didn't see my mother for fourteen years. I didn't know I had a choice, you see. When I came back, I spoke only English. My mother could not understand me, and I could not understand her."

From invasion to occupation

The final chapter in the repossession of Yakama lands occurred in 1887, when the Allotment Act was established as federal law. Popularly known as the Dawes Act, this federal policy remanded ownership of tribal land from collective to individual allotments, which were then "granted" to individual tribal members.

Under this policy, the tribe lost great swaths of land, as individuals were pushed from under the canopy of collective ownership into the free market economy. Upon the deaths of original allottees, the federal government claimed possession of all lands where there were no proven heirs. Descendants were required to prove their relationship to their parents, and since the law recognized only family relationships determined by official record, often church record, Native Americans who were not Christianized were often dispossessed of their homes. Many others lost allotments by way of trickery. Since many tribal members could not read or write, they signed documents signing ownership of their lands over to swindlers. My friend Herman recounted that his grandmother lost her allotment when she signed an X on an agreement with the grocer, an agreement she believed was an IOU for twenty dollars.

The primary purpose of the Allotment Act was to remove Indigenous Peoples from their lands. But it was presented by decision-makers as a kindness, a remedy for Peoples too "backward" to choose to assimilate into the dominant culture. Decision-makers argued that it was in the best interest of Indigenous Peoples to be separated from each other, to learn conventional agriculture, to compete with each other.

D. S. Otis, a historian commissioned by the Bureau of Indian Affairs to write a history of allotment under the Dawes Act, notes in his seminal work *The Dawes Act and the Allotment of Indian Lands,*

> That the White Man's way was good and the Indian's way was bad, all agreed. So, on the one hand, allotment was counted on to break up tribal life. This blessing was dwelt upon at length. The agent for the Yankton Sioux wrote in 1877: "As long as Indians live in villages, they will retain many of their old and injurious habits. Frequent feasts, community in food, heathen ceremonies and dances, constant visiting—these will continue

as long as the people live together in close neighborhoods and villages. . . . I trust that before another year is ended, they will generally be located upon individual lands of farms. From that date will begin their real and permanent progress."[3]

As the agent implies, placing Indigenous Peoples on reservations was not enough to break them. As long as they were together, they persisted in practicing their cultures, their traditional lifeways, and their spiritualities. The Allotment Act was overtly construed as a means of dividing sovereign peoples for their own good. In actuality, it stole 90 million acres guaranteed to Indigenous Peoples by treaty.

In the words of T. Hartley Crawford, the Commissioner of Indian Affairs in 1838, "Unless some system is marked out by which there shall be a separate allotment of land to each individual, . . . you will look in vain for any general casting off of savagism. Common property and civilization cannot co-exist."[4]

Under the Allotment Act, Indigenous-held lands in the United States were reduced from 138 million acres to 48 million acres.[5] Today, less than 13 percent of the people who inhabit the 1.4 million acres of the Yakama reservation are Native American; only 90,000 acres, or 6.4 percent, are held in trust by the tribe.[6]

Despite this history of dispossession and thievery, the Yakama people enjoy an incredibly proud and resilient society. In her book *Yakama Rising*, Michelle Jacob explores how the Yakama Peoples themselves have expressed resistance and self-determination throughout their history.[7] She lifts up activists and cultural practitioners today who persist in cultural traditions and provide healing and emergent solutions in the face of historical and ongoing trauma.

The Yakama Nation consistently exercises its sovereignty in defense of its lands and Peoples. Sovereignty is each tribe's inherent right to govern itself. While sovereignty may be an inherent right, it is constantly infringed upon by U.S. policy. Here are just a few instances of the Yakama Nation's resilience and courage in protecting their rights:

- They sought executive action to restore Pahto (Mount Adams) to Yakama control, resulting in Executive Order 11670, which restored 21,000 acres to the Yakama Nation in 1972.[8]

- They fought for preservation of traditional fishing rights guaranteed in the 1855 treaty, resulting in the historic Boldt decision in 1974.[9]

- They mobilized to stop the transit of nuclear waste across the reservation in 1979, a struggle that continues on to this day as the federal government seeks to reclassify nuclear waste that threatens the Columbia River, and tribal waters, lands, and health.[10]

- They defended their treaty rights to travel with goods for the purpose of trade, winning a Supreme Court ruling in their favor in 2019.

Beam (or trash) in the eye

When friends visit our home on the Yakama reservation for the first time, they often ask why there is so much trash in the yards of many of our neighbors. This is what I might have asked, too, when I was living in the dominant culture. My judgment of Henry and his beer can comes to mind.

Our family produces two neat cans of garbage per week; there is no local recycling program. Each can holds forty-four gallons, and together they weigh approximately eighty pounds. Using this estimate as our guide, our family of three generates about the national average of garbage each week.[11] For approximately twenty dollars per month, a waste disposal company comes each week to carry it away. No one need look at it or be inconvenienced by it.

Is the fact that our family can afford to have our garbage carted away a sign of our neatness, or goodness? Living here these past fourteen years, I have a different analysis: having trash in your yard is a function of poverty and systemic oppression. *Not* having trash in your yard is a function of privilege.

Do families who can't afford to have garbage carted away deserve scorn and judgment that they are being dirty, lazy, or wasteful? They don't demonstrably generate *more* garbage than others. Most of the Indigenous folks who live around here realize that their land was taken from them unjustly and that the beneficiaries of that theft live right here. Yet those same beneficiaries turn around and point to the ability to have trash removed as justification for *why we deserve the land. We* are neat, *we* are good people because we pay someone to carry our garbage away. *We* are good neighbors.

There is only one side

I ended up a settler here like everyone else, and yet . . . being a guest here has worked its way into my soul and changed me.

In the afternoon, I walk on the lane to the north field. Toppenish Ridge is to the south, resplendent in afternoon shadow. Pahto looms to the west, pure white though it is nearly summer. I walk the road across the wetland to the high grassy hill where we sled in winter, and I crouch down to wait. Still.

Still.

The wind is warm, gentle. My breath and pulse seem to synchronize with the pulse of the soil, and I feel it as I have many times before—the pulse deeper than words, the pulse of the world around me, the rhythm for all life. If I want to survive, I must work together with this rhythm, as does every creature on this land, from the microbes below to the blue heron beating its ancient wings above. Time does not slow, exactly. Rather, I sense true time—the rhythm of life. I see reality, that I am surrounded by the Spirit of Life.

My job, car, phone, television distract me from this reality. To survive, I must incorporate, collaborate with what is.

The fallacy of duality fades: Good or evil? Democrat or Republican? Legitimate or insurgent? Rural or urban? Free market or protectionist? Nuclear or coal? There is only one side: the side of Life.

Each spring, life returns to the soil in spite of humanity's best efforts. Though our community irrigates at a rate that leaches nutrients from the soil and depletes the aquifer; pours pesticides into biomes that disrupt the nervous system of pollinators; sprays herbicides that weaken the diversity of native plants; loads life-support systems of air, soil, and water with carcinogens—in spite of all of this, new shoots emerge from the soil, buds form on trees, animals return as the sun warms the fields, and water flows from snowmelt. We do nothing to earn this, and yet this renewal comes to us, free of charge. Grace.

A display at the Yakama Nation Cultural Center Museum proclaims: *In the beginning, the salmon people made a promise to man to provide food for him. Each year, they struggle to keep that promise.*

And another: *The hunter knows when he tracks his prey, it is his brother who waits for him.*

This is the promise of creation. In it we see the nature of the divine and the nature of grace—a gift unearned, undeserved.

I have been deceived into thinking I have a choice—that I can choose to live "sustainably," in symbiosis with this land, or I can choose to participate in systems that are destructive to it. What an infantile notion. There is only one side, and that is the side of Life and its systems. Anything that does not comply with the logic and rhythms of this delicate web is doomed.

What arrogance to believe that any one of us, or even all of us together, can thwart the systems of Life. Its rhythm has been heard in space since the beginning of time. The heartbeat of this earth is ancient and will go on long after our civilization, and the next. If there is a struggle, it is for our own survival, but there are no sides.

The forces of darkness, the principalities and powers that seek advantage and short-term gain, favor force, crush the vulnerable for profit, and follow the logic of extraction and all its divisive processes, are doomed. Their logic is a logic of death. There is no argument, no technological advance that can expand the capacity of a fragile human lung, or platelet, or skin cell. How fabulously foolish to believe any system invested in the destruction of creation, the Ancient of Days, will stand.

This is what I have learned from living here as a guest on the Yakama reservation for fourteen years. I can cooperate, co-create with the systems of Life, which is my only choice, or I can pass away and waste my life following the hollow logic that leads to death. Jesus' call to the fishermen to lay down their nets and follow him was an invitation to participate in the endless cycle of Life. Answering Jesus' call to work for justice, which brought me to live in community on the homeland of the Confederated Bands and Tribes of the Yakama Nation, has also opened me to more fully understand both the cosmology of my own ancestors[12] and the meaning of Jesus' call. Finally, I understand the cryptic words of Paul, who writes, "And the world and its cravings are passing away, but the person who does the will of God remains forever" (1 John 2:17).

THREE

Is Everyone at the Table Who Needs to Be Here?

IN NOVEMBER 2013, I found myself somewhere I never expected to be: at the 10th Assembly of the World Council of Churches in Busan, South Korea. Not only was I attending, but I had worked with other Indigenous leaders for two years prior to the assembly to ask the largest ecumenical organization on earth to stand with Indigenous Peoples in dismantling the Doctrine of Discovery. To do that, I sought the aid of my fellow peace church delegates, who were Mennonite, Quaker, and Church of the Brethren. I had become a Mennonite by conviction years earlier because I was drawn to the teaching and example of people who believed in radical peacemaking—in choosing systems of Life over systems of death—and in following Jesus wherever he led.

Now I stood before these delegates, asking them to help me and seventy other Indigenous church leaders pressure the World Council of Churches (WCC) to intentionally oppose resource extraction on Indigenous lands and to actively negotiate for peace on behalf of displaced and marginalized Indigenous Peoples. The time for "symbolic solidarity" had passed, I argued. I had been assured the peace churches would stand with us.

Now that commitment looked doubtful. A prominent Mennonite theologian urged his colleagues not to listen to me. "This assembly is too important for us to be distracted by one issue," he said.

"We are not an issue," I responded, "but a People, with a message of hope for humanity." For the church to allow extractive industry—systems of death—to continue to destroy the earth's life-support systems for short-term profit would make the earth uninhabitable for us all. For the body of Christ to stand by and watch the most vulnerable sacrificed first, without comment, was unthinkable, I argued.

This prominent theologian felt we were a distraction from the work of peacemaking; I argued that, as peacemakers, we were calling the church to resist the structural violence so many Indigenous People around the world face. The peacemaking theologian prioritized diplomacy and negotiation as an alternative to organized violence like war. We advocated for a broader definition of peacemaking, where the systemic violence that ultimately culminates in armed conflict is named and confronted.

Saying yes, again

The story of how I came to stand before the delegates of the WCC in 2013 began when Maria Chavez, an Indigenous Bolivian theologian and organizer who staffed the Indigenous desk at the WCC, sent out a plea to member churches in

2011, asking them to encourage the WCC to repudiate the Doctrine of Discovery. I received her forwarded plea from a friend named Doug Hostetter. Doug had accompanied Dan on the first Mennonite international human rights delegation to Suriname several years earlier, where he had photographed the impacts of mining on Indigenous communities. As the Mennonite Central Committee representative to the United Nations, Doug was forwarded Maria's email by the chaplain at the Church Center for the United Nations in New York.

Doug forwarded Maria's email to me because he had experienced the beauty and suffering of our partners in Suriname firsthand. He included a short note, asking if working with the WCC might help us. Dan encouraged me to reach out to Maria. "What will I say to her?" I asked him. "I'm not a theologian or even a pastor."

I sent an email to Maria anyway, offering to help. "I don't know what help I can be," I admitted, "but if I can provide support on a team, I am happy to try." Maria wrote back to me right away, arranging a Skype conversation. I was shocked by her quick response. She was based at the WCC headquarters in Geneva, Switzerland, while I was in rural central Washington State, many time zones away.

Within the first few minutes of our conversation, Maria told me that I was the only person of the 350 member churches who responded to her missive. "Draft a statement and bring it to the WCC," she urged me.

"Me?" I asked. "I'm not a theologian, Maria. Why don't you hold a conference for theologians and come up with a statement?"

She smiled at me sadly. "We don't have the money for that, or, frankly, the time. You know this, Sarah. There is suffering that must not wait for theologians to make up their minds. Besides, none of them responded. You responded."

"But, Maria! Why don't you write the statement? You have the experience, and the training."

"But the WCC won't listen to me. As staff, it's inappropriate for me to try to shape institutional priorities that should come from the people," she told me. "They will listen to you. You have responded to the call. It must be you."

"Tell her yes," Dan whispered from across the room.

I closed my eyes and gritted my teeth. "Yes, I will do it," I said.

I wrote to theologians and called others, asking for help. None responded. Out of desperation, I reached out to Robert J. Miller, a Native legal scholar and expert on the Doctrine of Discovery. I had met him at a book signing at the Yakama Nation Cultural Heritage Center, shortly after he published *Native America, Discovered and Conquered: Thomas Jefferson, Lewis and Clark, and Manifest Destiny*. He agreed readily. He then in turn recruited John Dieffenbaker-Krall, who had written the first repudiation statement on behalf of the Episcopal Church, and Steven T. Newcomb, a Native history scholar and expert on the Doctrine of Discovery. Oren Lyons, elder and national Indigenous leader, agreed to advise.

The statement took months of work. We engaged in extensive research and met via teleconference regularly. Each member of the team brought specific expertise to our bimonthly conference calls in which we spent hours discussing and revising the statement. In addition to the writing, I also spent months lobbying and organizing to bring it to the attention of the WCC Executive Committee. Maria encouraged me all the way. I often felt I was not qualified to convene the calls, author the statement, or call on the largest ecumenical body on earth to change course. Maria urged me, "If not you, then who? You answered the call. You can do it."

Ultimately, it took the collaboration of Indigenous People around the world to write the statement and get it before the executive committee. I met many amazing people. One Indigenous man I knew by phone but had never met, Harley, even flew to a nearby city to get the statement into the hands of an executive committee member. In the end, we were successful! The WCC Executive Committee adopted the statement with no significant changes.

Maria, my stalwart friend and supporter, died of cancer before the statement was adopted.

Our 2012 statement brought to the attention of the WCC Executive Committee the fact that the well-being and existence of Indigenous Peoples are threatened by an ongoing program of colonization, including laws and policies that amount to forced assimilation. We pointed out that "the patterns of domination and oppression that continue to afflict Indigenous Peoples today throughout the world are found in numerous historical documents such as Papal Bulls, Royal Charters and court rulings. . . . Collectively, these and other concepts form a paradigm or pattern of domination that is still being used against Indigenous Peoples."[1]

Although these documents directing European explorers were written more than five hundred years ago, we acknowledged that legal precedent around the globe which originated with the Doctrine of Discovery has resulted in current laws in "almost all settler societies around the world today."[2] Specifically, our statement spelled out that the WCC Executive Committee

a. expresses solidarity with the Indigenous Peoples of the world and supports the rights of Indigenous Peoples . . . ;

b. denounces the Doctrine of Discovery as fundamentally opposed to the gospel of Jesus Christ and as a violation of the inherent human rights . . . ;

c. urges various governments in the world to dismantle the legal structures and policies based on the Doctrine of Discovery and dominance . . . ;

d. affirms its conviction and commitment that Indigenous Peoples be assisted in their struggle to . . . exercise their right to self-determination and self-governance;

e. requests the governments and states of the world to ensure that their policies, regulations and laws that affect Indigenous Peoples comply with international conventions . . . ;

f. calls on each WCC member church to reflect upon its own national and church history and to encourage all member[s] . . . to seek a greater understanding of the issues facing Indigenous Peoples, to support Indigenous Peoples in their ongoing efforts to exercise their inherent sovereignty and fundamental human rights . . . ; [and]

g. encourages WCC member churches to support the continued development of theological reflections by Indigenous Peoples which promote Indigenous visions of full, good and abundant life and which strengthen their own spiritual and theological reflections.[3]

Once the statement was adopted, I wondered what action the WCC was prepared to take that would bring about the changes we articulated were necessary—action that, in short, would dismantle the Doctrine of Discovery. I was then to learn that the adoption of this statement would result in only one action: the WCC would post the statement on their website.

It felt like a slap in the face. I had worked on the statement because I was asked to, and because I was appealing to the largest body of Christians I could find, petitioning them to stand with Indigenous Peoples globally in resistance to the oppression that binds us, that dehumanizes us. What I had hoped for was an institutional commitment to stand up to the powers that continue to violate our rights as human beings—specifically, by opposing resource extraction on Indigenous lands. Instead, the institution, the most representative church body on earth, understood what was happening to us and was choosing to do nothing about it.

Next stop: Busan

I refused to accept this as the final word from the WCC. I wanted to turn this "unfunded mandate" into a program that could be enacted. In a great example of what true partnership looks like between settlers and Indigenous People, an anonymous donor offered me a small grant that made it possible for me to drop to part-time at my paid job for six months. Mennonite Central Committee's Indigenous Visioning Circle recommended me to this donor. This gift, I found out later, was made possible when the donor received his inheritance from the sale of his family farm. He understood his family's land had been wrongfully taken from Indigenous People, and he resolved to use it to fund Indigenous Peoples' work.

With the flexibility this gift afforded, I researched WCC Indigenous member churches and reached out to their leadership. At Indigenous gatherings that the WCC hosted in Geneva and New York, I held side meetings with these Indigenous leaders, and together we strategized how to lobby the WCC to make an institutional commitment to dismantle the Doctrine of Discovery. We met by phone monthly, with representatives from North America, South America, Central America, Australia, West Papua, Europe, the Pacific region, and India. An institutional commitment to dismantle the Doctrine of Discovery would require permanent staff and program funding, we reasoned. We sought a codified mandate for an Indigenous Peoples' program, an institutional commitment to this work, and a structural process to accomplish it.

In the 1980s, the WCC had housed a similar program, called the Programme to Combat Racism (PCR). This small and mighty program, which was established in the late '60s, had championed the end of apartheid in South Africa, bringing vital moral authority to the demand to end the institution of apartheid. We could do this again, we felt, by creating a program to end the Doctrine of Discovery. Specifically, we asked that the WCC

- establish a vigorous network of Indigenous church and lay leaders, activists, NGOs and theologians;

- voice and affirm an alternative worldview where decisions are made collectively and the well-being of partners is valued over agendas or outcomes;

- acknowledge the threats to life voiced among Indigenous Peoples suffering the impacts of extraction and climate change; and

- acknowledge, affirm, and multiply the growing movement toward engaging the powers of this world in negotiation for justice. In the words of Mark MacDonald, the National Indigenous Anglican Archbishop for the Anglican Church of Canada, "The church must muster more courage than at any time in history to resist the forces of destruction that threaten life itself."[4]

We drafted a resolution we hoped the WCC would adopt, and developed a plan to bring this document to the assembly in Busan. Although the agenda for the 10th Assembly had already been set, we agreed that we would work to have our statement read on the delegate floor and request its inclusion in the institutional priorities.

I went on a speaking tour of Europe with Jacob, a Dutch Mennonite who had accompanied Dan on the human rights delegation to Suriname. Our task was to urge WCC member churches in Europe to advocate for the adoption of policy to dismantle the Doctrine of Discovery. Everywhere I spoke, church leaders agreed that they would help us in Busan. Allyship seemed assured.

A few nights before the assembly was to convene, I received an email from Iris, a Dutch friend and delegate, informing me that the peace churches were to meet in an hour. I was surprised that I had not been contacted by the organizers of the meeting, since I had made many contacts in Europe during my travels and felt confident that the peace churches especially would support the Indigenous delegates at the assembly. I rushed to the meeting by cab and sat down to find a strategy session already in process to address their collective issues. They had several statements pending about conscientious objectors and just peace, but nothing about the resolution brought by myself and other Indigenous leaders. During the conversation, I realized that they had been working together to strategize for many months, were well organized, and were using their influence to get their issues heard. However, they had known for a year that I was coming to the 10th Assembly with a delegation of Indigenous leaders, and they had not included us in their planning.

Further, I had specifically asked a prominent theologian of the traditional peace churches for help when I had been in Europe. He had assured me he would help us, but I had not heard from him for many months. In fact, Iris had told me the day before that I needed to "tone it down." He did not want to work with me, she said, because I was "just an activist." This had stung, but to also learn that the allies I had been counting on had intentionally sidelined me was devastating. I had believed that both the Dutch church and this theologian were supportive of our efforts. It was one thing to be marginalized by the WCC. It was another to be marginalized by those I believed would help us.

A staff member from the WCC, Joe, spoke up in the meeting and said, "All we are talking about is process. Where is the conversation about justice?" Iris asked why the Indigenous resolution had not been included on the agenda. I did not speak, but I started to cry. I felt tired and ashamed. I had worked very hard in the dark, believing I had found allies who would help my people. The strategy the peace churches were describing was not the strategy I had been advised to use. Although at the time I thought the prominent theologian I mentioned in the beginning of this chapter was helping me, I believe now that he was dismissing me by providing small pieces of incomplete information as an afterthought. Whether or not that was his intention, that is what it felt like to me, and the outcome was the same.

At the next meeting of the peace churches a few days later, I came prepared.

I demanded to be on the agenda and that fair time be allocated to each statement that was pending. I said that the group had betrayed the trust of the people who had sent me, most importantly the vulnerable I represented. By not including us in the emails, organizing, information, and support, they had marginalized us. Specifically, I asked for

- a consensus vote from the group that they would take up the resolution and support it as one of their primary issues;
- delegate votes;
- advice and support from committee members (since four Anabaptists sat on decision-making committees);
- inclusion in all future strategy sessions; and
- support from potential WCC Central Committee members.

As we were leaving the meeting, a white Quaker woman who was sitting on a crucial decision-making committee at the WCC told me, "You know, no one in this group is trying to marginalize you, and no one at the WCC is trying to marginalize you."

I told her, "I would be happy to have this conversation with you if you like, but it merits more time than two minutes on the way to the bus. Since you are in a position of power, I understand why you would say that. But I will just point out that that is what the powerful always say to and about the marginalized."

It would have been much more helpful to me if this woman had said, "You have a point of view I haven't heard.

I'm distressed about it. And, in my position of power, I want to make sure that I can hear your voice fully. Would you be willing to meet with me and talk?" This would have signaled to me that she was willing to put in the time to listen about how I had felt marginalized, rather than engage in a rather dismissive one-minute conversation, and that she was open to learning about processes of marginalization within the WCC of which she might be unaware. I wouldn't necessarily have expected her to agree with me, but I do expect and hope that my experience as an Indigenous woman can be taken seriously.

Of course, many people feel that being cordial is good enough, and that cruelty is measured by active, individual bad behavior. The reality is that choosing *not* to include the vulnerable has the same effect—dismissal—and being passively dismissed amounts to marginalization. The marginalized have little voice. They must be *actively included*. A failure to include is de facto exclusion.

I am the Canaanite woman

As he listened to me recount my humiliating meeting with the peace churches, my friend Ken, an Aboriginal church leader from Australia and a delegate to the WCC Assembly, explained to me the story of the Canaanite woman from Matthew 15:21-28. Jesus is with his disciples when he is approached by a Canaanite woman who asks for healing for her daughter. She names Jesus, saying, "I know who you are, and what you are capable of." Jesus denies her request, saying he has come only to help his own people. His disciples tell him to send her away. She does not take no for an answer and gets in his way and demands his help. He tells her, "It is not good to take the children's bread and toss it to dogs." She endures this insult and persists in her demand for help. It is here that Jesus is confronted with his own biases. The woman, through her actions, is saying to him, "I demand that you deal with me. Are you really who you say you are?" She presses on, getting in his way, enduring two denials and being called a dog. But finally, Jesus grants her request, calling her a woman of great faith.

"You are that Canaanite woman," Ken said to me. "She had the power to confront even Jesus, and call him to account for justice."

Ironically, I was at the WCC Assembly to persuade the global church to take on the role of the Canaanite woman. The church has the moral authority to call extractive industry, Western governments, and economic development institutions into direct negotiation with Indigenous Peoples struggling for their survival. This was the peacemaking the coalition of Indigenous leaders and I longed for. For us, this would have meant true solidarity.

In the end, our Indigenous statement *was* heard and adopted unanimously by the delegates in Busan. But the Indigenous Peoples' program never materialized. Although a position related to Indigenous issues existed at the WCC, administrators who managed the hiring process required that the person staffing the program have a PhD in theology. Potential staff would be required to live in Geneva, potentially thousands of miles from home communities. The education requirement excluded Indigenous church leaders who lived in regions or economic conditions where a PhD was out of reach. It also excluded experienced Indigenous organizers who could mobilize a global base. The program was effectively intellectualized.

Additionally, once an employee was hired, she was directed to split her time between the Indigenous program and another global program. For either program, it would have been impossible for one staff member to do all the work required to develop and direct an effective program. For a single person to manage two global programs meant one program would necessarily be sidelined. In fact, when I visited New York in 2018 for the United Nations Permanent Forum on Indigenous Issues, I met with the WCC United Nations' liaison. She told me, "I think it would be great if the WCC worked on Indigenous Peoples' issues. To the best of my knowledge, we have never had such a program." The Indigenous program had been so marginalized within the institution that this staff person was unaware of its existence.

Indigenous Peoples are excluded from the decision-making table because excluding us advantages those in power, and because including us involves changing "how things are done." Providing us "voice" by occasionally publishing an essay by an Indigenous theologian or providing a day of prayer will not do the job of protecting the precious and vital systems upon which we are all dependent—water, soil, and air. Joining Indigenous Peoples in our struggle as we agitate for the lives of our communities, and for the survival of humanity, requires risk.

In the case of the WCC, spoken solidarity gave way to the reality that donor churches from developed nations prefer programs that benefit themselves, where activities include largely symbolic and intellectual actions like conferences, printed resources, and prayers. As often happens, this self-correcting institution resisted the challenge and call that Indigenous Peoples posed and reaffirmed the status quo instead. Those in power—which in the WCC often means Western churches—are also unwilling to confront extractive industries because of the considerable funding such industries provide them. Like secular institutions, faith institutions are invested in oil, gas, and precious metals for revenue and for retirement funds, which is a topic I will cover more fully in chapter 7.

What we asked the WCC to do may seem radical, audacious. We asked the body of Christ to actively seek justice by engaging the powers in direct negotiation with Indigenous Peoples. This felt risky and continues to feel risky when many churches depend on income from extractive industries. Yet radical peacemaking is at the heart of Christ's call.

When I was talking with a secular activist earlier this year, she told me, "I don't know what you expect; the church is a conquered people. They have signed a treaty with the state, and for staying out of trouble they get their tax exemption." My experience with the WCC and other church bodies has made me wonder, sadly, if perhaps this is true.

FOUR

The Doctrine of Discovery and Me, Again

I **MET MAX IN 2013** when she took a sociology course I
taught at Heritage University, a private Indigenous-serving
university located on the Yakama Indian Reservation. Max was
mostly reserved during that first course, but when she spoke,
she asked insightful questions that challenged her classmates
and me. After that first course, she registered for my classes
multiple times. We got to know each other over her undergrad-
uate career.

Max is smart and curious, and has a particular incisiveness
that disarms those around her and opens dialogue. She is not
one to back down when faced with an opposing opinion, even
a forceful one. But when discussion turned to tribal matters or
Indigenous issues, she became reserved and detached. When I
mentioned to her in a private conversation that I had observed

her withdraw from conversations relating to Indigenous issues, she told me that while she was an enrolled tribal member, she did not know how to "keep traditional." She admitted that this felt shameful to her. "I don't know how to do any Indian stuff," she told me. "I don't know the stories. I don't know the religion. So I just keep my mouth shut." She cried quietly as she told me this.

Max was not the only student who recounted these sentiments. Several young women I had relationships with during my years at Heritage shared the same feelings. "I don't have a grandmother," one young woman told me. "My mom grew up in foster care." "I grew up with my dad," explained another, "and he is from Mexico." Each time a student or friend admitted they "didn't know" about their culture, it was with a sense of shame.

As I began speaking about the Doctrine of Discovery around the country, select attendees would stay afterward, waiting to be the last to speak with me. These folks would hang around the outskirts of conversation looking for a private moment. They would then explain a genetic Indigenous heritage without a sense of how to connect. Shame was invariably conveyed, as well as a sense of being an outsider.

Soon, I began to see a trend reminiscent of a diaspora—a longing to connect without an understanding of how. "I am afraid to reach out to my tribe," one woman shared with me at a congregation in Southern California. "They don't know me because my dad didn't grow up on the reservation. I don't know anything. I don't even know how to get in touch with my relatives." A feeling that you have to "know how" to be a Native American was repeated to me again and again. "I must not be Native, because I can't claim a reservation, a language, or even relatives," a man in the Midwest confided in me. These words were invariably accompanied by embarrassment and the humiliation that I might accuse them of being pretenders.

The humiliation expressed struck a visceral chord. I saw my own humiliation in their faces, in the eyes of both students at Heritage and those who waited to talk with me at engagements across the country. I had grown up with shame, with a sense that some vital piece of myself was missing, and that I did not belong.

A legacy of shame

Throughout my years in school, I felt a deep sense of shame. I was insecure about my family's poverty and about my shyness and social awkwardness. As a small child, I was often teased for my dark skin and Native facial features. My appearance, coupled with hand-me-down clothing, made me a frequent object of ridicule.

When I was a teenager, my family shared a two-bedroom apartment with another family; six of eight people who lived there were children in middle and high school. I slept on the floor in the living room. I kept my few personal possessions in a cardboard box. I never had more than one pair of shoes and rarely more than one change of clothing. I worked as a housecleaner, and my hands were cracked and swollen from the daily use of industrial cleansers. My household was the scene of frequent fights between teenagers forced to share space, and brutal punishments handed out by adults. I lived in fear of violence, and I had no privacy. Many nights I went to sleep hungry.

At school, I joined choir because I loved the peace and sense of togetherness that singing in a group provided to me. I loved choir practice. The music room was a safe place where my voice could fit in, where my voice was one strand in harmony with the group. The collective voice of the choir was beautiful to me, so much more than my voice alone. Together, we produced beautiful music that seemed to emerge by magic.

But when it came time for performances, I was late, or I missed them all together. I could not drive, our family was often without a car, and chaos at home determined whether or not I would even be allowed to walk or take the bus to a performance. I would not ask for a ride from another student, because I didn't want anyone to see where I lived. After missing multiple performances, other choir members ridiculed me for letting the team down. I quit choir, unable to explain to my teacher what was happening at home.

During college, I distanced myself from my family. I worked hard to speak correctly and assimilate into the dominant culture. I created anecdotes to provide cover when friends asked about my family or childhood; I envied my friend Jessie from Canada, who had no family nearby and therefore did not need to make explanations during holidays when families typically gather. I felt depressed and sometimes desperate, and I isolated myself. I often had nightmares and flashbacks, making it difficult to sleep. I persistently experienced thoughts about my worthlessness, and I toyed with the idea of suicide. I felt exhausted. I could not imagine a life where I would ever feel better. I believed that I was somehow defective and that I didn't deserve to feel happy.

I buried these feelings in work and achievement. I worked full-time in college to support myself while concurrently enrolled full-time. I sublimated my fears and dark thoughts in work. It was not unusual for me to work at multiple jobs and then study for several days in a row without sleeping. These periods were followed by days of exhaustion, where I would stay isolated in my apartment. I felt wracked with social anxiety and a belief that no one would ever really love me.

Mental health counseling helped me get through this difficult time in my life and enabled me to envision a future for myself. I made a decision to break with my past and just look forward. While I loved family members I had grown up with, it was simply too painful to be around them. I moved overseas, then across the country to attend graduate school. I reasoned that my parents were dysfunctional people, but I didn't need to live in the shadow of their mistakes. Living in a city where I knew no one, I could create my own identity.

When Dan and I moved to the homeland of the Confederated Bands and Tribes of the Yakama Nation, I began teaching at Heritage University, where I met Max. Many of the Native students who grew to trust me confided in me that they experienced feelings of hopelessness similar to those I had experienced when I was in school. As they shared their stories with me, stories which often included poverty, abuse, and neglect, I found that they were very similar to mine. At first, I thought that a few students with a similar history felt drawn to me. But as years went by and I got to know more and more students, I realized that my story was mundane; it was nearly identical to those of many of my students. As I began to learn about the Doctrine of Discovery, I realized that this shame was born of trauma intentionally inflicted by my country.

A legacy of intentional trauma

In his book *Native America, Discovered and Conquered: Thomas Jefferson, Lewis and Clark, and Manifest Destiny*, legal scholar Robert J. Miller describes distinct eras of United States Indian policy designed to permanently remove Indigenous Peoples from their lands by way of war, violence, forced relocation, internment, land-grabbing, urbanization, segregation, and discrimination.[1]

During the Trade and Intercourse era (1789–1825), the United States established policy to govern trade and political discourse with Indigenous Nations and to ensure that only the federal government could control Native American lands.[2]

The Removal era (1825–1850s) established policies as the final solution to the "Indian Problem," by forcing the Indigenous Nations in the eastern United States to relocate west of the Mississippi River.[3] This solution was hardly final. The Gold Rush in California, the expansion of the Oregon Trail, and the resolution of the Mexican-American War in the late 1840s meant a flood of American settlers rushed to the Western territories.

The Reservation era (1850–1887) resolved to force Indigenous Nations onto small, remote reservations established by treaties negotiated under threat of violence by the U.S. military. Reservations were much smaller than Indigenous tribes' traditional food-gathering areas, often outside their traditional homelands, and resources for adequate food, medicine, housing, clean water, and other necessities were inadequate. These necessities continue to be inadequate for tribal peoples in the United States today.

As discussed in chapter 2, the Allotment and Assimilation era (1887–1934) further diminished Indigenous lands by reducing the size of reservations that treaties had established. To break up tribal ownership of land and open reservations to American settlers, reservations were divided into small allotments, which were then assigned, or "allotted," to individual tribal members.[4]

The U.S. senator who proposed the legislation, Henry Lauren Dawes, famously explained at the Lake Mohonk Conference:

> The head chief told us that there was not a family in the whole Nations [one of the Five Civilized Tribes] that had not a home of its own. There was not a pauper in that Nation, and the Nation did not owe a dollar. It built its own capitol . . . and it built its schools and hospitals. Yet the defect of the system was apparent. They have got as far as they can go, because they own their land in common. It is Henry George's system, and under that there is no enterprise to make your home any better than that of your neighbors. There is no self-ishness, which is at the bottom of civilization. Till this people will consent to give up their lands, and divide among their citizens so that each can own the land he cultivates, they will make no more progress.[5]

Allotments were historically impractical for Indigenous Peoples and remain impractical today because they are based on the assumption of land cultivation. Imposed on Indigenous Peoples who followed their own cosmologies and economies, a small square of land that did not provide access to the diverse materials needed for survival was baffling. For example, many Indigenous Peoples in the Pacific Northwest depend on salmon as the primary source of protein. A small allotment of dry land that does not provide access to a river cannot provide the food necessary for survival.

Once all Indigenous lands had been allotted to tribal individuals, any remaining land was considered "surplus" and sold to American settlers without the consent of the Indigenous communities. The policies resulting in allotment dissolved collective ownership of land by Indigenous Peoples. Once land was privately owned by Indigenous individuals, it was easily taken by banks, state governments, and individuals, often fraudulently. Bureau of Indian Affairs (BIA) agents, the federal administrators of reservations, frequently failed to provide farming equipment to Indigenous land allottees, which meant Indigenous farmers could not support themselves on the land they owned. Many allottees sold their land simply to buy food. Previously on reservations, collective land ownership had made it possible to hunt, fish, and gather food on a common land base. Allotments made this impossible.

The Allotment Act was designed to break up contiguous Indigenous lands, thereby weakening tribes and their governments. Reservation lands today have a "checkerboard" quality, where Indigenous-owned parcels are punctuated with the parcels of non-Native owners. Sometimes dozens or even hundreds of descendants of an original allottee share claim to a small parcel of land. Population growth has thus made it impossible for many contemporary Indigenous families to remain on their land.

Forced assimilation was another objective legislated during the Allotment and Assimilation era.[6] The federal government tasked Christian denominations with operating the primary institutions on reservations, including missions, schools, and even the BIA office. Boarding schools were created to Christianize and assimilate Indigenous children, who were forcibly removed from their parents' care and institutionalized in schools where disease, malnutrition, neglect, assault, and abuse were rampant. James Smith, a historian from the Yakama Nation, explains that children were required to learn a foreign language (English), abandon their life-sustaining religion, and assimilate to the American culture.[7] As BIA agent of the Yakama school Robert Milroy explained, "Indian children can learn and absorb nothing from their ignorant parents but barbarism. Hence the vast importance of detaching them from their parents as soon as they reach school age."[8] Such boarding schools in the United States were supported by national legislation from 1819 to 1973. Many people do not know that these boarding schools persisted in the United States even through the 1980s and 1990s.

During the Termination era (1940s–1961), official U.S. policy was to terminate the legal existence of tribal governments permanently, and effectively end "Native American Identity."[9] The logic was that Indigenous People were thought to be American citizens, just like everyone else, and thus treaties were anachronistic. The elimination of tribal governments also meant more loss of land that had been held in trust by those governments. While termination was formally reversed in 1988 with the end of House Concurrent Resolution 108, the U.S. government set criteria by which tribes must now prove their legitimacy to be federally recognized. Many tribes lost federal recognition under these policies and are still unable to meet the criteria to be recognized. According to the U.S. Department of the Interior, there are seven mandatory criteria to establish a "nation to nation" relationship with the United States:

a. it [the petitioning group] has been identified as an American Indian entity on a substantially continuous basis since 1900;

b. a predominant portion of the petitioning group comprises a distinct community and has existed as a community from historical times until the present;

c. it has maintained political influence or authority over its members as an autonomous entity from historical times until the present;

d. it has provided a copy of the group's present governing document including its membership criteria;

e. its membership consists of individuals who descend from an historical Indian tribe or from historical Indian tribes that combined and functioned as a single autonomous political entity, and provide a current membership list;

f. the membership of the petitioning group is composed principally of persons who are not members of any acknowledged North American Indian Tribe; and,

g. neither the petitioner nor its members are the subject of congressional legislation that has expressly terminated or forbidden the federal relationship.[10]

Actions taken by the federal government have made meeting these criteria difficult if not impossible; many tribes have been dispersed as a matter of policy. Forced removal of tribes from their homelands, as in the Trail of Death the Potawatomi people endured, detaining children in boarding schools, and relocating individuals and families to urban areas are all examples of actions that have effected a diaspora that makes it difficult for a people to "function as a single autonomous political entity." These criteria also assume a level of enfranchisement that has been denied to many Indigenous people. How could a dispossessed people struggling for survival keep an accurate record of membership?

As the federal government sought to reduce Native American subsidies that had been defined by treaty, shrinking the population of reservations became a primary aim.[11] The Indian Relocation Act (1956) created programs to relocate Indigenous individuals and families to cities. Indigenous individuals were promised paid relocation, vocational training, medical insurance, assistance in purchasing a home, and funds to purchase relevant equipment to enter a trade. An estimated 750,000 Indigenous People migrated to cities during this era. Many Indigenous individuals who entered the program were not provided the promised services and found themselves jobless, homeless, and hundreds of miles away from their support systems and homes. In cities, they were isolated and faced a high cost of living, discrimination, and segregation.

When I began to learn about the Doctrine of Discovery and all that it means for Indigenous and tribal peoples in the Guiana Shield, I began to notice the similarities between their story and my own as an Indigenous woman in the United States. Because their lands in the Guiana Shield are rich in minerals, timber, and other coveted sources of wealth, Indigenous Peoples are pushed out. They are frequently driven into urban areas without material wealth or access to a lifeway, or else are forced to live in highly contaminated areas without access to food, healthcare, or electricity. This parallels the formation of reservations in remote locations in the United States—which were often created on the poorest lands that were too small to support the population—as well as the policy to urbanize Indigenous families.

In Suriname, children must move to urban areas to receive education beyond fifth grade. They are housed in boarding schools hundreds of miles from their families. There are frequent reports of mental, physical, and sexual abuse in boarding schools. Suicide of students is frequent, both at schools and among young people when they return home. This parallels the mandate for Indigenous children to be placed in boarding schools in the United States, where they were separated from their families and unable to speak their own language or practice their own culture or spirituality, often from early childhood through their teen years.

The lasting legacy of boarding schools

The legacy of boarding schools has made a particular impact on my life, as it has for so many Native people in the United States and Canada. In Canada, the Truth and Reconciliation Commission estimated that 3,200 Native children died in residential schools over a span of 120 years. At the time of the commission's final report in 2015, among the 70,000 former residential school students still alive, there were 31,907 verified cases of sexual abuse or assault. We do not have current records in the United States documenting deaths and cases of abuse in our boarding schools.[12] But boarding school survivors recount stories of hunger, abuse, neglect, and death.

My father, a Pueblo (Tewa), never knew his mother—he was removed from his people at birth in 1943. He grew up in a home for Native American boys and was subject to habitual abuse, forced labor, and malnutrition. He was not one of the exceptions who was able to rise above his conditions. As his daughter, I grew up subject to abuse, homelessness, and hunger. Like many Indigenous People in my generation, I came to understand my own story in middle age, through the truth and reconciliation process that took place in Canada.

I met Chief Wilton (Willie) Littlechild in New York City at a WCC expert consultation in conjunction with the annual United Nations Permanent Forum on Indigenous Issues. Chief Littlechild, a Cree attorney and former member of the

Canadian Parliament, was there as one of three commissioners of the Truth and Reconciliation Commission of Canada.

About a dozen of us sat in a small space in the Church Center for the United Nations, in a room just big enough for the conference table at its center. A lifelong athlete, Chief Littlechild is a tall, muscular man with a proud bearing. He filled the room, dwarfing the setting. Although he spoke quietly, the rest of us were overwhelmed by his presence and the power of his words.

He began by telling us about the furs and boots that were made for the children of his village by their parents to protect little bodies against the winter in the extreme north. These were taken and burned by school administrators when children were taken into compulsory residential schools. They were deemed the garments of savages. The children were given cloth coats and shoes, inadequate against harsh winters. Braids were cut from the boys; siblings and even neighbors were separated; tribal language was not to be spoken, and to violate this norm was to be faced with corporal punishment. Indigenous spirituality was mocked and forbidden.

All of this I knew already, had read and heard. But the visual image of the piled-up boots and coats was chilling. Chief Littlechild explained that these children knew viscerally that their comfort and protection was being stripped away. I could picture the piles of warm clothes heaped next to lines of exposed, humiliated children shivering in their Western clothes. Many would not see their families again until they were eighteen. Many would not be able to communicate with their parents when they returned home, since they were conditioned to speak only English and would not have the skills to survive in their Native communities. Chief Littlechild endured this; he explained that he had been one of these children. He had watched his own leather and fur boots burn, the ones his mother had made for him. It was painful to witness the grief of a large and imposing man, a leader of his people, as he described a childhood of abuse and deprivation at the hands of the state.

Chief Littlechild then began to tell us about the thousands of testimonies he had witnessed as a commissioner of the truth and reconciliation process. He recited the numbers of children who had died in residential schools. Of malnutrition. Of exhaustion and overwork. Of bodily injury from abuse. Of influenza and other viruses inadequately treated. Of criminal neglect. Many parents were not informed that their children had died. Even when they were informed, they were not given their children's remains. The Truth and Reconciliation Commission went about the macabre work of searching for the tiny bodies buried in unmarked graves on residential school grounds.

Chief Littlechild's voice cracked as he described testimony after testimony where men stood and explained that they had never talked about what had happened to them. Their stories of horror had rotted inside them. Many believed their parents would come for them and grew bitter waiting. Those who tried to run away were tied to their beds and beaten more severely for each attempt. Again and again, he heard fathers and mothers explain that they had never told their children "I love you," because they were incapable of feeling or expressing love. Others explained how they had hurt their own children with either the constant rage they walked with or emotional distance they could not bridge. Many shared struggles with substance abuse and depression. Many wept openly, unable to control what had never been told before, sobbing so hard they could not speak. You can watch these testimonies on YouTube. They are crushing.

As Chief Littlechild spoke softly into that small room, the volume of his stories was deafening. I wept silently. I wanted to run from the room and probably would have if I'd had the space to maneuver around the awkward conference table. I wanted to cover my ears. For the first time, I understood my own story clearly. So much of what Chief Littlechild shared of the testimony of survivors—the abuse, neglect, cruelty passed on to children—was the experience of my childhood. And I understood for the first time that my suffering, that the suffering my father had endured growing up an orphan on a farm that was part of a Catholic "boys' home," was an outcome of U.S. domestic policy.

My own history came into focus in a social context. My shame about my own abuse had caused me to sublimate it—to blame it on my dysfunctional parents who refused the American dream, and to try to create a life in the dominant culture by denying my past. Now I saw that I was not alone. Since boarding schools in the United States existed until the 1990s, many Indigenous People my age and older grew up in boarding schools. Most of the people my age and older that I know on the Yakama reservation grew up in boarding schools, without hope.

Like Max, many people like me had been raised by traumatized parents who had been separated from their families, communities, cultures, and the wealth of their Native lands. My father had been removed from his family at birth and grew up three hundred miles from his Native community. His labor was considered inadequate recompense for his board; he endured malnutrition, neglect, and abuse. Like many Native men traumatized by abuse and separation from his family, he repeated these behaviors with his own children.

Like many Native children, I hid my own poverty and abuse, believing it was my fault. As an adult, I saw assimilation into the dominant culture as my path out of misery, moving to a distant city to get as far away from my childhood as possible. As an adult I began to see that this was the intention of the boarding schools; I was following a predictable path set in motion by the U.S. government in 1819 with the Civilization Fund Act.

Without access to my Native land, community, extended family, culture, or spirituality, my past held only shame that I wanted to distance myself from. How many Indigenous and tribal children in the Guiana Shield will survive the "historical" process now taking place in their own lands? Theft and contamination of their lands. Consolidation of communities into areas that cannot support them. Removal of children to boarding schools. How many offspring will survive this violence of attrition, this genocide? Of the survivors, how many will make the choices I planned to make, for assimilation?

Can you see that the Doctrine of Discovery is not a historical concept but a current juggernaut with predictable ends? The Doctrine of Discovery is a system of laws and policies meant to permanently remove Indigenous Peoples from the birthright of their lands and wealth by force: genocide, relocation, urbanization, and forced assimilation. A tiny number of Indigenous People survive the battering of generations and the loss of this birthright, and many choose assimilation as though it is their own idea. Like I did.

The story of Jacob and Esau

In my Sunday school classes as a child, I remember learning about Abraham's descendants and especially about the ones God blessed. In the story of Esau and Jacob,[13] I learned that Esau was impulsive and unable to plan ahead, while Jacob was patient and clever. Jacob was able to obtain his hairy (uncivilized), hotheaded brother's birthright just by providing some stew and bread to Esau. This felt to me like a reasonable cautionary tale, much like Goofus and Gallant from *Highlights* magazine. Goofus misbehaves; Gallant does what he's asked. Goofus complains about brushing his teeth (and gets cavities); Gallant does it without being asked (and has healthy teeth). Goofus sleds into traffic without looking (and is in danger); Gallant looks for a safe place to sled (and remains safe). Goofus eats the cookies set aside for guests (and gets in trouble with his parents); Gallant reminds him that the cookies should be saved and shared later (and is praised). Jacob has his act together; Esau loses his birthright because he doesn't.

In Sunday school, I shook my head at Esau's foolish impulsiveness with the rest of my class. In retrospect, through an Indigenous lens, I see another story. As an Indigenous woman, I see that I am in the position of Esau, not Jacob. The fool who has lost her birthright.

The story explains that Esau, a "man of the open country" (uncivilized), loses his birthright to his brother Jacob, who "stays among the tents" (civilized). In a moment of Esau's desperation and hunger, Jacob manipulates Esau, providing him food in exchange for his birthright.

Jacob is clever and scheming, and is rewarded for his cleverness again and again. He deceives his aged father in a successful bid to receive the blessing his father, Isaac, intended for Esau. He gains this unethically, in addition to Esau's birthright, which he has already taken. He does this for power and material gain.

In the story, Jacob is the protagonist who is blessed by God, while Esau is the fool.

In Romans 9, Paul explains that God's elect are justified by God, and we need not look for explanations:

> Not only that, but also Rebecca conceived children with one man, our ancestor Isaac. When they hadn't been born yet and when they hadn't yet done anything good or bad, it was shown that God's purpose would continue because it was based on his choice. It wasn't because of what was done but because of God's call. This was said to her: *The older child will be a slave to the younger one.* As it is written, *I loved Jacob, but I hated Esau.* (vv. 10-13)

This logic of the elect provides theological justification for the lost birthright of Native America. In the European migration to the New World, the people of God, the Christian elect, are justified to take what they will.

The Doctrine of Discovery was designed to remove Indigenous Peoples from their lands. Tonya Frichner, Special Rapporteur to the Permanent Forum on Indigenous Issues, explains the intention of the papal bull we heard about in chapter 1, *Romanus Pontifex*, this way:

> The papal bull *Romanus Pontifex*, issued in 1455, serves as a starting point to understand the Doctrine of Discovery, specifically, the historic efforts by Christian monarchies and States of Europe in the fifteenth and later centuries to assume and exert rights of conquest and dominance over non-Christian indigenous peoples in order to take over and profit from their lands and territories. The overall purpose of these efforts was to accumulate wealth by engaging in unlimited resource extraction, particularly mining, within the traditional territories of indigenous nations and peoples. The

text of *Romanus Pontifex* is illustrative of the doctrine or right of discovery. Centuries of destruction and ethnocide resulted from the application of the Doctrine of Discovery and framework of dominance to indigenous peoples and to their lands, territories and resources.[14]

In the landmark 1823 Supreme Court case *Johnson v. M'Intosh*, Chief Justice John Marshall wrote the majority opinion that shaped laws and policies toward Indigenous Peoples in the following way:

> On the discovery of this immense continent, the great nations of Europe were eager to appropriate to themselves so much of it as they could respectively acquire. Its vast extent offered an ample field to the ambition and enterprise of all; and the character and religion of its inhabitants afforded an apology for considering them as a people over whom the superior genius of Europe might claim an ascendency. *The potentates of the old world found no difficulty in convincing themselves that they made ample compensation to the inhabitants of the new, by bestowing on them civilization and Christianity*, in exchange for unlimited independence. But, as they were all in pursuit of nearly the same object, it was necessary, in order to avoid conflicting settlements, and consequent war with each other, to establish a principle which all should acknowledge as the law by which the right of acquisition, which they all asserted, should be regulated as between themselves. This principle was that discovery gave title to the government by whose subjects, or by whose authority, it was made, against all other European governments, which title might be consummated by possession.
>
> The exclusion of all other Europeans, necessarily gave to the nation making the discovery the sole right of acquiring

the soil from the natives, and establishing settlements upon it. It was a right with which no Europeans could interfere. It was a right which all asserted for themselves, and to the assertion of which, by others, all assented.

Those relations which were to exist between the discoverer and the natives, were to be regulated by themselves. The rights thus acquired being exclusive, no other power could interpose between them.[15]

As I read Marshall's words, I find myself asking if we are truly intended to follow Jacob's example. To me, this story is a cautionary tale: Jacob betrays his father and his brother for his own self-interest and amasses great wealth; following the example of their father, out of their own self-interest, Jacob's sons sell his favorite, Joseph, into slavery; Joseph then ascends to a position of power in Egypt and advises the pharaoh to use a terrible famine to his advantage and buy all the land, resources, and enslaved bodies of his citizens in exchange for grain, essentially making Pharaoh like a god; a few generations later, the entire nation of Israel is enslaved to the absolute power of the pharaoh; to escape their bondage, Israel commits genocide . . . and on and on. To my mind, this story was recorded so that humanity could see the insanity of Jacob's behavior and choose to turn away from systematic violence, toward the justice the prophets cried for.

Yet these stories have been used to justify the seizure of Indigenous Peoples' lands and continue to perpetuate a mythos of elect entitlement and manifest destiny. In the Christian telling of the settlement story, the church is the protagonist, following Jacob's example and blessed by God. My people are the fools, the heathens.

Chief Justice Marshall succinctly explains the position of colonizers who presume they are taking the place as the elect, justified by their status and their desires: "The measure of property acquired by occupancy is determined, according to the law of nature, by the extent of men's wants, and their capacity of using it to supply them."[16]

This is the logic of Jacob.

Marshall's opinion continues:

> It is a violation of the rights of others to exclude them from the use of what we do not want, and they have an occasion for. Upon this principle the North American Indians could have acquired no proprietary interest in the vast tracts of territory which they wandered over; and their right to the lands on which they hunted, could not be considered as superior to that which is acquired to the sea by fishing in it. The use in the one case, as well as the other, is not exclusive. According to every theory of property, the Indians had no individual rights to land; nor had they any collectively, or in their national capacity; for the lands occupied by each tribe were not used by them in such a manner as to prevent their being appropriated by a people of cultivators. All the proprietary rights of civilized nations on this continent are founded on this principle. The right derived from discovery and conquest, can rest on no other basis; and all existing titles depend on the fundamental title of the crown by discovery. The title of the crown (as representing the nation) passed to the colonists by charters, which were absolute grants of the soil; and it was a first principle in colonial law, that all titles must be derived from the crown.[17]

When I read the logic of Jacob in the chief justice's ruling—a logic that forms the basis for U.S. domination of Indigenous

Peoples—I realize that my people and I are neither fools nor heathens. The dominant culture's logic is reductive, extractive, and about domination. The shame is not mine.

What if we were to behave as if this story were a cautionary tale, instead of seeing it as containing instructions for how we are supposed to live? If this is indeed a cautionary tale, then what would that mean for us as the church?

FIVE

We Don't Need Help, We Need Relatives

I MET THE CREE ELDER Stan McKay at an expert consultation on the Doctrine of Discovery hosted by the World Council of Churches in 2012.[1] I was in New York attending the United Nations Permanent Forum on Indigenous Issues, and Stan and I were on a delegation of about a dozen Indigenous leaders gathered to reflect on the Doctrine of Discovery in the context of the UN and the global church.

Stan told us that the image of truth held by the church, with its "commitment to the exceptionality of humanness," has been too small. Shouldn't truth include all of creation?

"There was a Creator of earth among us before the Western story came," Stan told the delegation. He said mission should be "an exchange of good news, a theology of life." He said, "We don't need help, we need relatives." Stan had a powerful impact on me. Both his words and his presence moved me profoundly. He spoke with authority. His words had power.

At a dinner after our delegation's first day together, I squeezed into a seat next to him and asked if I could talk with him. "I am so angry, all of the time," I told him. "I don't know how to deal with this work on the Doctrine of Discovery. I feel it burning inside of me. I don't like it, but I don't know how to make it stop."

All my past came spilling out of me. The violence and poverty I grew up with. My ambivalence about my Native identity, given my lack of tribal affiliation. My anger at the church, historical and present, for the wrongs done to my people and my friends. My bewilderment at being called to work on the Doctrine of Discovery, and its weight, pulling me into darkness. And the resulting despair and anger. I was traveling around the world, with a baby son waiting for me at home. I felt guilty for every hour I spent away from Dan and our son. I felt driven to seek justice on behalf of my partners in Suriname, who as non-Christians had no position in the church, who needed allies and had, from my point of view, a poor one: me, a rural mother trying to solve a tangled ball of twine the size of a mountain in her "free time." I had not at that time, and still have not to this day, held a paid job in any church body, which means I have a full-time job and use my vacation time to pursue the work of the church.

All of this spilled out at that public dinner. Stan was kind to me despite my outburst. He told me that I needed healing, and he advised me to return to my homeland, the home of my grandmother, to seek healing in the sacred waters there. "Trust the water," he told me. I am a different person for having followed his counsel.

In his essay "Living in the Shadow of *Doctrine*," Stan writes:

North American Church mission is flavoured by colonial history. I feel the activity of proselytization should cease until the people of the Church (both Settler and Indigenous) comprehend how the Doctrine of Discovery presently influences them. The churches also need to engage in their own healing because all of society has been impacted by an unjust history, and we continue with the historical struggle to this day.[2]

I am guided by Stan's assessment of mission.

The great commission

The great commission is said to have been a primary justification for the genocide that killed most of my people, and the slow process of assimilation that followed. It is found in the gospel of Matthew:

> Now the eleven disciples went to Galilee, to the mountain where Jesus told them to go. When they saw him, they worshipped him, but some doubted. Jesus came near and spoke to them, "I've received all authority in heaven and on earth. Therefore, go and make disciples of all nations, baptizing them in the name of the Father and of the Son and of the Holy Spirit, teaching them to obey everything that I've commanded you. Look, I myself will be with you every day until the end of this present age." (28:16-20)

Jesus, the Christ, has risen from the dead. Women go to his tomb, meet an angel, and according to his instructions, tell the disciples to meet Jesus in Galilee. This passage ends the book of Matthew; the prophecy has been fulfilled.

The text is very specific. It says to teach everything I have commanded you. What does Jesus command his disciples?

Love one another (John 13:34-35). Love God with all your heart; love your neighbor as yourself; love your enemies (Matthew 5:44-45). Don't retaliate. Don't harbor anger, but seek reconciliation. Give to the needy. Forgive those who trespass against you. Don't judge others. Don't commit adultery. Don't worry.

I do not hear a command for world domination. Yet this text in Matthew, through the systems of the church, has empowered Christians to colonize the world.

Forced conversion is justified by the Doctrine of Discovery. William Galbraith Miller, a nineteenth-century legal scholar, describes this process in the following way:

> Christendom is now the unity, of which Christ's vicar on earth is the head, and the crusaders give a practical direction to this idea, while on the theoretical side, at a later date, it is worked out by the Spanish and the Dutch jurists. They divide mankind into (1) believers, (2) infidels and heretics, and (3) heathens. International law, which is tacitly or expressly assumed to be the private civil law of Rome, applies to the first. Toward the second [category], war is the normal and proper attitude; and as to the third, if they do not at once accept the Gospel when offered, war is justifiable.[3]

As Miller notes, the consequence of not accepting the "good news" is war.

The Requirement

The Requerimiento, or the Requirement, was a document read to Indigenous People from the boats of Spanish colonizers coming to claim their lands. This document explained the legal and spiritual justification for the seizure of their lands. As Spanish soldiers came to claim the New World, a priest would read out the legal justification for the invasion according to this narrative: God, the Creator, mandated one man, Saint Peter, as the lord and superior of all men on earth, and all people should obey him. Saint Peter was the first pope, whom God commanded to be the judge and governor of all the people of earth. Over generations, the first pope had been succeeded by others, who were each affirmed as the ruler of the world in his stead. One of these popes had made a donation of the lands inhabited by the Natives to the king and queen of Spain. The Natives were therefore notified that they were to submit to the rule of the king and queen because the sovereigns had been assigned the legal rulers by the representative of God (the pope). The Native people were asked in the Requirement to submit to this rule. If they would not, the consequences would be dire:

> If you do not [submit to this rule], . . . with the help of God, we shall powerfully enter into your country, and shall make war against you in all ways and manners that we can, and shall subject you to the yoke and obedience of the Church and their Highnesses; we shall take you and your wives and children, and shall make slaves of them, and as such shall sell and dispose of them as their Highnesses [the king and queen of Spain] may command; and we shall take away your goods, and shall do you all the mischief and damage that we can . . . and we protest that the deaths and losses which shall accrue from this are your fault, and not that of their Highnesses, or ours, nor of those cavaliers who come with us.[4]

The invaders' practice of installing a priest to read the requirement was truly a farce, since it was read in Latin from the invading ship as the Spanish disembarked. Even if the people on shore could hear them, they could not understand Latin. Many Natives were slain and enslaved, a process justified by the international laws of the time, which were established in Rome, where the church served as the author and arbiter of international law.

The Requirement is one small piece of the early execution of the Doctrine of Discovery, grounded in the papal bull *Dum Diversas* of 1452. I note it here because it is an expression of the lived embodiment of the colonization justified by the great commission.

I understand that almost no one today would agree with the tenets of the Requirement or the way it was executed. I do not bring it up here to hold people in the dominant culture today responsible for this historical justification for genocide. I do want to point out that elements of the logic contained in the Requirement are embedded in how mission continues to be conceptualized. From my perspective, three central concepts in the Requirement remain part of the logic of mission:

1. The creator God has sent members of the church who are empowered to make things happen in the lands of Indigenous Peoples.

2. Indigenous Peoples are subordinate and must submit to the authority of missionaries.

3. Missionaries are frequently the emissaries of a political power, in league with the state.

1. The creator God has sent members of the church who are empowered to make things happen in the lands of Indigenous Peoples. Many people who sit on mission boards, as well as donors who fund mission, do not see anything wrong with this paradigm. Missionaries are sent to "help" for the "good of the people," and recipient communities are the objects of mission. It is assumed that since the action is "ordained" and the workers are sent by God, whose intentions are good, no evil will result from bringing outside influence, expertise, technology, goods, and services to foreign or even domestic Indigenous communities. This assumption alone is the source of anger and resentment among many Indigenous People.

One close friend in the United States responded to me with frustration over the constant flow of mission groups coming to his reservation to help with building and home repair programs. "They are taking jobs from local people," he told me in frustration. "I have told missionaries they are displacing workers here, but they don't seem to care."

The assumption that mission work is always helpful and necessary means that mission workers are often ignorant and heedless of how their efforts can upturn all aspects of community life in Indigenous communities. In the rainforest in Suriname, the arrival of missionaries has challenged how youth relate to their parents, who is authorized to make decisions, who or what sits in the assumed position of absolute authority, how work is to be conducted, how food and resources are to be shared. All of these fundamental aspects of social cohesion and socialization were fundamentally disrupted by missionaries who assumed what they had to offer was not only "good" but *better* than what the communities already had.

In a rainforest community with whom Dan and I have a relationship, all food and work were shared in common before the arrival of Westerners, who brought with them a money-based economy. Just fifteen years later, many men had left the village for paid employment, leaving collective work undone. Neighbors stood by as their fellows went hungry, and homes of the less fortunate went unprepared for monsoon season. The social cohesion of the village was in utter disarray. I saw poverty and hunger in that place for the first time as the people were brought into the money-based economy.

When armed with the assumption that God has empowered them to "make things happen," missionaries also misinterpret local resistance to their outside intervention.

When Dan and I were invited to work with communities in Suriname, not as missionaries but as public health researchers, the Matawai and Saramaka people we interacted with refused to provide hair samples to colleagues who were trying to discover the impact of mercury contamination on individual health. Our colleagues did not understand why, until one man, Jimmy, explained his reluctance this way: "You are going to take part of my body away and do something with it in secret. I don't know where you are taking it, what you are going to do with it, or what effect that will have on me." I was struck during this conversation by how true his statements were. Although researchers planned to put his hair through a photon spectrometer to measure mercury contamination, a seemingly benign action from a clinical viewpoint, the outcome would certainly have consequences for him and his community. His government did not want the impacts of mining contamination to be known to his community, and therefore researchers had no intention of relaying the data to Jimmy or his community. In essence, they would analyze his hair, draw conclusions from it, and do all of this in secret. They would make decisions that would affect him without his consent or input.

Colleagues from the public health arena at the time felt frustrated with Jimmy's response, however, believing it to be a reaction of ignorance and superstition. "They think we are going to perform black magic on the hair," one colleague voiced in annoyance. "They don't understand the research is for their own good." This paternalistic sentiment dismissed the real consequences to community members who might participate in these health studies. In my own life, I know I would not willingly give a part of my body to strangers without knowing what the process for diagnosis would be and without promise of that diagnosis being shared with me.

2. Indigenous Peoples are subordinate and must submit to the authority of missionaries. The public health examples I offered above may seem distinct from mission work, but they are imbued with the same assumptions of hierarchy and superiority that lead not only to resentment but to actual damage in Indigenous communities. The papal bull *Inter Caetera* (1493) was the foundation for the Requirement, and it explained the authority given to the invaders who came to conquer and colonize in the name of Christ. Submitting to the authority of the missionary, God's messenger, is consistent with submitting to the authority of God, even as conversion was intertwined with colonization.

Because Christian missionaries still bring with them a worldview in which failure to convert to Christianity will mean eternal damnation, their message and mandate to follow the great commission supersedes the authority and will of the Indigenous Peoples they encounter. Today, missionaries may not see themselves as conquerors or agents of the state. However, their ability to exist and flourish in Native lands requires the cooperation and goodwill of political authorities. This goodwill carries consequences with it, and Indigenous Peoples are damaged by this arrangement. Missionaries and those who send them comply with the authority of the state. For Indigenous Peoples, on one side lies the authority of the colonizing authority, including the military. On the other is the church, bearing the authority of the Almighty. Indigenous Peoples are faced with the threat of eternal damnation on one side and invasion on the other. Force and violence are at play in both instances, and submission seems the only choice.

3. Missionaries are frequently the emissaries of a political power, in league with the state. Reminiscent of the Requirement, missionaries often arrive in Indigenous lands with the aid and support of state and military power. Jacob Loewen, a missionary from the Mennonite tradition, attempted to "modernize" mission by incorporating anthropological analysis into the work of the mission field.[5] In a 1965 paper describing mission in small tribes in Latin America, Loewen states:

> In Latin America, national governments have frequently encouraged mission organizations to work with tribes in hopes of "civilizing" them and eventually incorporating them into the national society. A number of countries have signed concordats with the state church turning over tribal groups to religious orders for "civilizing and Christianizing them."[6]

Here is another example Loewen offers in the context of the Mopass Residential School in Northwest Canada:

> Christianity was "given" to the Indian by means of the churches and church schools, as a primary acculturative pathway. In all of the contact period and down to the present times, churches were the chosen instruments for "dealing

with" the Indians. . . . The Whiteman was—and is—willing to give his idealized moral order to the Indian. Indeed, he is quite insistent about it! He was not—and he is not—willing to give political and economic power to *anyone* if he can keep it for himself.[7]

Loewen's approach was quite progressive for his time, in that he believed missionaries and their tactics could be observed and evaluated based on "objective" analysis. However, the collaboration with state power that he benignly observed in the articles cited above can still be seen in the Guiana Shield and, I have no doubt, in other parts of the world. Regardless of their individual intent, the missionaries come with the full power of colonization and domination by the state. Any message of Jesus they hope to share is eclipsed by the reality: removal, relocation, starvation, war, and death perpetrated by colonization.

Missionary collusion with state authorities also happened in the United States in the form of boarding schools that were engaged by the U.S. government to divide children from their parents and "civilize" them. The Yakama Nation museum engaged James Smith, a Yakama historian, to document some of what happened at the Yakama boarding school at Fort Simcoe.

U.S. government officials, known as Indian Agents, regarded Yakamas a people requiring liberation from their former "barbarous ways." This belief required drastic action. The Yakamas needed to learn a foreign language, abandon their life-sustaining religion, and take up a new lifestyle to fit with the "Great Father's" intentions for them. Agents worked to make the Yakamas thrifty, industrious, Christian wards that would make their living as farmers and artisans. In short, the Yakamas were to give up their lifeway for a new one. To accomplish this aim, federal officials naturally focused on the Yakama children. Officials believed that if Native Americans were to be "saved," their children had to conform to the new order.[8]

As mentioned in chapter 2, James Wilbur, a Methodist missionary known as "Father Wilbur," served as the first Indian agent at the Fort Simcoe boarding school.[9] The *Oregon Encyclopedia* describes him in this way:

> In keeping with the contemporary attitudes, Wilbur was dismissive of traditional Native culture. He treated Indians like children who needed lessons of "the bible and the plow"— Christianity, education, and physical work—in order to "wake up from the night of sin to the Gospel day and glorious hopes of future bliss." Wilbur favored Methodist converts with houses, jobs, and federally issued goods, and he was reprimanded for not equitably distributing the treaty-mandated goods. He intimidated Catholic Indians, barring their priests from the reservation, and he jailed leaders of the native Dreamer religion.[10]

In keeping with the Civilization Fund Act of 1819, whereby Congress funded Christian missions to administer boarding schools in the United States, Wilbur ran the school as a Methodist mission. Today, the local Methodist church in White Swan, where my family and I reside, still bears his name: Wilbur Memorial Methodist Church. Regardless of contemporary trends in missiology, the impact of Wilbur on the reservation where I live is ongoing.

Impact of mission in the Guiana Shield

Regardless of the intent, the impact of mission has been devastating to my partners in Suriname and French Guiana. In the 1960s, the government of Suriname initiated Operation Grasshopper to open up the interior by clearing airstrips in the forest at strategic locations where mineral exploration seemed promising.[11] A Baptist mission organization was granted permission by the government at the time to establish itself among the Wayana. The missionaries consolidated Wayana villages into large communities, and these communities would receive education and medical treatment and engage in trade.

Population concentration was a policy of these missionaries in order to efficiently provide medical and pastoral care. But we can presume that the state also benefited from this village consolidation. In efforts to survey the interior rainforest, which is rich in mineral wealth, the Suriname government has claimed that most of the interior region is "empty" of people and therefore available for resource exploitation.

In their evaluation of the sustainability of livelihoods among the Wayana, the Amazon Conservation Team remarked, "Today, almost all Wayana are Baptist and this religion dominates social and cultural life. As a result, traditional dances, songs, stories, cosmology, and other cultural expressions are rarely practiced and unknown by Wayana children. Some shamans are still active as healers but no longer publicly perform rituals involving association with the spirit world."[12]

From the perspective of missionaries, what has happened with the Wayana is a source of pride. According to Charles, a man who spent periods of his childhood living among the Wayana with his family, his missionary grandparents sacrificed their family's comfortable American lifestyle in order to reach the hostile Wayana tribe that had "little previous contact with the outside world." They created the Wayana's written language, taught them how to read and write, and translated the Bible into their language. They claim with pride that the Wayana no longer live in fear of evil spirits. In her exploration of conversion among the Trio and the Wayana in Suriname and French Guiana, Vanessa Grotti states, "To the missionaries, shamanism and shamanic practices were associated with the Devil and his agents, which take the form of spirits."[13]

However, when the Wayana describe the conditions in which they are forced to live, they describe how they no longer have any sort of future in their traditional tribal family, how they are excluded from the democratic market system, how many people have become inconsolable and have given up. Social oppression and prejudice from members of the dominant culture contribute to the trauma of assimilation and to the stressors causing many people to commit suicide.

In May 2017, a young Wayana woman named Cecilia, a fifteen-year old schoolgirl attending boarding school took her life. In response, officials dispatched a helicopter and a medical team. "Was [dispatching a helicopter] a good thing?" asked village leader Armand, who is president of a local Indigenous NGO that supports and defends Amerindian and Native American children. "Will this team [of medics] be able to fix the suicide epidemic?" A community leader told us missionaries claim that Cecilia committed suicide because of the sins of her parents. According to the missionaries, her parents were unsaved.[14]

A week later, another suicide was reported in the area. As Dan wrote in a press release, "The drastic change in culture, customs, and social institutions that results from economic development programs forcing the Wayana to accept a Western democratic market-based lifestyle is hard for young people and that depresses them. They no longer have landmarks to guide them, and young parents and elders do not understand the 'new way.' They have no answers."[15]

In May 2019, Dan and I received an email from Miriam, an in-country partner in French Guiana, describing her despair at the number of suicides taking place in forest villages among young people. "We are again in sadness. Amanda, a young Wayana, pregnant, is given to death yesterday. The seventh suicide in 6 months. This is carnage!"[16]

While early missionaries provided material support for Wayana communities, I have been told by elders that such help stopped long ago. Now, church groups mobilize the Wayana to engage in mining activities so that they can earn income to pay for the mission.

Meanwhile, Jaque, a community leader of a village in French Guiana, explained to us that he participates in Christianity because he is afraid of the consequences if he does not. "They [the missionaries] are the ones that have a voice in the life of the community now. If I don't participate, they will act without input or supervision." In a village with whom we have been in relationship for many years, there is more than one mission outpost. The two groups are at odds with each other, and families are divided over which group to affiliate with. A young woman committed suicide while we were visiting in 2015 because she was, according to her boyfriend, "heartbroken over the division of her family."

Wayana youth find themselves without hope. Paul, an eighty-five-year-old elder, recalled that "the Wayana people used to live in harmony, happy and proud. We lived in community," he said. "People woke up early imitating hawk songs. The men went hunting or fishing and the women went to search for cassava, pineapples, and yams. In the evening families gathered around the fire. Suddenly, modern schools and modern religion arrived. New foods. And strong alcohol and drugs, too. These things have upset the Wayana way of life." Most of Paul's brothers (fellow elders) regret these changes but say it is too late to turn back.

I return to Stan McKay's sense that evangelization to Indigenous Peoples is wrong at this time. The mission to the Indigenous Peoples that I have observed in the rainforest in the Guiana Shield is either a misguided dream that is tragically failing in its primary intent or a crime that is achieving its primary intent.

Witchcraft or good news?

I experienced Winti spirituality in working with tribal people of Suriname. The Maroon people are the descendants of escaped slaves who established isolated rainforest communities during the era of the slave trade (1667–1863), where thousands of workers in bondage worked on the coastal plantations.[17] As enslaved Africans escaped into the forest, they established or joined traditional communities, practicing the culture, spirituality, and traditions of their native African lands. Tribal peoples inhabit the interior rainforest region of the Guiana Shield alongside Indigenous Peoples.

Like the Peoples indigenous to Suriname, Maroon communities are also affected by mining. While some are Christianized, many continue to practice Winti, what is described as an "Afro-Caribbean" religion. Winti means "wind" and "spirit" in the national language of Suriname, Sranan Tongo. Henri Stephen, a health administrator who has incorporated tribal healing into the application of public health in Suriname, describes Winti this way: "Winti represents, when taken as a whole, the power of the unseen elements in the atmosphere which rule our lives. . . . The two main characteristics of Winti are its connection with the ancestors and its relationship with nature."[18]

This is what I have learned from my experience working with Maroon people. In Winti cosmology, individual agency is only part of what makes up reality. If a problem is experienced, it could be because of "what came before" —that is, because of a problem that really occurred in the life of an ancestor. When conflict emerges between people in a village, it may require ceremony to invoke preceding generations to engage in resolution.

It is believed that hatred is powerful enough to kill an enemy. Hatred must be addressed, or it could lead to death. Sometimes entire family groups must engage in ceremony to heal a conflict between two individuals. It may also be necessary to engage in ceremony that calls the ancestors from both family groups into resolution together.

An individual's choices are important because they may create problems for future generations. According to the same logic, an individual's choices are not the only thing that shapes reality, because the choices of those who came before also have an impact on the present. The feuds of ancestors may be causing problems for the individual now. In the Winti cosmology, one's actions are influenced by those who came before and have the power to hurt those who will come after. It is therefore important for individuals to understand themselves as part of a web of generations—those who came before and those who will come after.

In small, isolated communities, peace is essential for the survival of the community. Dealing with conflict is a serious matter. Hatred is not taken lightly. This understanding is profound for peacemaking in any tradition.

When I began to build relationships with Maroon people, I was closed to learning about Winti, which had been described to me as "witchcraft." In my own North American spiritual upbringing, any tradition that was non-Christian was heathenism. What I learned in relationship with warm, kind, and loving friends is that Winti embodies a spiritual cosmology that is an opportunity for redemption for Americans like me.

According to the American cultural lens, the individual is the creator of one's own reality. The self is the center of reality. A primary assumption is that if a person is in crisis, it must be because of something the person did. Likewise, if someone has power or wealth and chooses to waste resources or pollute an environment, these are individual choices. There is very little tolerance in the individualist American culture for understanding historical causes or historical trauma, including how our choices contribute to the trauma those in the future will face.

Winti, on the other hand, places the self not at the center of reality but in a web that includes the past, the present, the future, and the natural world. Individual actions have consequences for generations. An individual is acting on the natural world while also being shaped by the natural world. As in many Indigenous traditions, reverence, or an acknowledgment of one's place in the cosmos, is a key practice.

I am by no means an expert on the intricacies of Winti. But learning about it has been redemptive for me. It has influenced my thinking about peacemaking, which must include the past and the future; structural violence, my role in it, and therefore my responsibility to repair it; and climate change and how small actions, when taken across billions of lives, equate to disaster for all of creation.

It has had a powerful impact on my relationship with the Creator, because the premises of Winti that I describe above are consistent with Jesus' mandate and the vision of restoration for all of creation. I truly learned about Jesus' call from women who showed me love, Winti practitioners, in the rainforest in Suriname.

Whose souls need saving?

I want to point out here that my elders and teachers may be shocked and dismayed at my open call for the church to change its behavior. Who am I to tell you what to do? Unfortunately, I am not wise enough to softly explore this topic in a good way. I apologize, and I humbly submit to you some ideas for how things might be different.

> Be careful that you don't practice your religion in front of people to draw their attention. If you do, you will have no reward from your Father who is in heaven.
>
> Whenever you give to the poor, don't blow your trumpet as the hypocrites do in the synagogues and in the streets so that they may get praise from people. I assure you, that's the only reward they'll get. But when you give to the poor, don't let your left hand know what your right hand is doing so that you may give to the poor in secret. Your Father who sees what you do in secret will reward you.
>
> When you pray, don't be like hypocrites. They love to pray standing in the synagogues and on the street corners so that people will see them. I assure you, that's the only reward

they'll get. But when you pray, go to your room, shut the door, and pray to your Father who is present in that secret place. Your Father who sees what you do in secret will reward you. (Matthew 6:1-6)

In this passage of the Sermon on the Mount, Jesus is teaching humility to his disciples and the crowds who have come to hear him. The mission I have described above is not about humility; it is about conquest. In the quest to "save souls," these missionaries have shamed and divided the families they are there to minister to, have set them up to compete with one another, and have drawn community members into mining activities that are detrimental to individual and community health. The missionaries' primary aim appears to be the health and success of their own institutions rather than the health of the communities to whom they are offering "salvation."

Elisabeth Elliot, a missionary who lived with the Aucas in Ecuador in the late 1950s, is famous for taking the post of her husband after his death at their hands. In her memoir, *The Savage My Kinsman*, she states,

The Auca . . . knows nothing of drunkenness or wife beating. He may kill his neighbor, but he does not fight with him. He may not participate in any community projects, but he shares his one small monkey with the widow next door. He may practice polygamy, but he faithfully supports all of the wives he has. He does not greet a friend or bid him good-day, but he entertains without charge any guest who happens in, even if he is a Quichua Indian whom he has never seen. He does not wear clothing, but he has a strict code of modesty and is totally free from the American preoccupation with the human body, and all of the absurd inhibitions this involves. In short,

I was faced with the fact that socially I had nothing whatever to offer the Aucas. Any comparison between myself and them, from this standpoint, was painful to me. Why was I here? There was no answer but the simplest, most elemental: Jesus Christ. To obey him, to present him.[19]

Elliot acknowledges the lifeway of the Auca and the ways in which her own culture falls short. But she goes on to dismiss these realizations in favor of her "mission." Her memoir makes it clear that she has a spiritual truth to share that will "save" the people she is there to evangelize. She believes that she has something to share with them, Jesus, that will save their souls, which is more important than what she has learned about the social ways of the Auca. She does not even consider that the Auca have an understanding or experience of the Creator that, if shared, could save hers.

You may believe Elliot's views are old-fashioned and out-moded, and that we don't do mission in the same way today. But what I see in the rainforest of the Guiana Shield follows the same logic Elliot expresses: supremacy. *I know what the good news is, and you are the object of my good news. You do not have any spiritual good news to share with me. There is nothing you know about the nature of the Creator of the universe that may be redemptive for me.*

This paradigm for mission is not only offensive but tragically malformed, incomplete. What redemption is missed by missionaries and the Christian church by a stubborn commitment to affirming one face of the Great Unknown?

What is the good news? To learn this, we must explore it *together.* Salvation must be mutual, and entangled. My salvation is tied to yours. Yours is tied to mine. From my point of view, the Indigenous and tribal peoples I have described in this chapter are not in jeopardy of losing their souls. But those of us in the developed world who benefit from the threats to their existence may be in jeopardy of losing ours. Should we ask them to teach us so that we can turn away from evil, like the king of Nineveh in the book of Jonah who repented when confronted with God's judgment?

If we are able to humble ourselves as Christians and seek to learn how to see the cosmos—to truly see it and our place in it—as our Indigenous relatives do, perhaps there are those among us who would benefit from mission. Let us send missionaries to mining interests, to oil companies, to banks. Let us prepare missionaries and send them and their families for commitments of thirty years or more. Let us endeavor to learn their language, to translate the gospel into a context they can understand. Those pulling the levers of the system of death may be in jeopardy of losing their immortal souls. Should we not minister to them?

Why not send missionaries to the United Nations, to the U.S. Treasury? Let us learn their ways, their thinking. Let us call them to repentance. Not in a statement. Not in a press release. Let us send missionaries to build outposts, let us embark on a program of conversion. Let us win these souls to Christ and his mandate. Let congregations support families, pictured on bulletin boards, who are working in New York, Geneva, Washington, D.C., Toronto. Let us have annual days of prayer for those working in the vineyard, harvesting workers for the kingdom, in the places of power that threaten life for all of creation.

Please do not mistake this suggestion for hyperbole, or as a whimsical dig. I really mean it. Our institutions are empowered to define mission, to equip mission, to send workers to the vineyard. What would mission look like through an Indigenous lens? Restoration for creation. Redemption for those managing the levers of the forces of death. I am serious about sending missionaries to the mining and oil companies, to the principalities and powers. Perhaps through relationship, the individuals working in these systems might yet be saved. Perhaps through relationship with spiritual workers, these institutions might be brought to repentance. Then, like the king of Nineveh in the book of Jonah, leaders of these institutions might call for repentance. In the words of the king of Nineveh in Jonah 3:9, "Who knows? God may see this and turn from his wrath, so that we might not perish."

SIX

Reimagining Our Theology

I HAVE DESCRIBED MY JOURNEY with the Doctrine of Discovery as analogous to Frodo Baggins's journey carrying the ring of power to Mordor. In the iconic trilogy *The Lord of the Rings*, a small, humble Frodo must cross continents filled with perils and countless enemies to dispose of the ring of power, which has a hold over all of Middle-earth. He must go to the stronghold of the enemy and throw the ring into the fires of the mountain where it was forged. The ring is evil. The ring is heavy. With each step, the weight of the burden grows heavier. The burden of carrying the Doctrine of Discovery, for me, has been confronting the evil that I have been taught is part of the message of the Creator, and which has had a hold over Christian theology as it has been practiced for five hundred years. I must name this evil, and attempt to dispose of it in the heart of the lie where it was forged.

I am talking about confronting genocide justified by Christianity. The exodus story is itself a story of genocide.

I say this knowing that the exodus has been the basis of an entire canon of liberation theology and that many peoples claim this story as liberating. I want to be sensitive to the original tradition of the Hebrew Scriptures—the Jewish tradition. I want to underline that the narrative explored here is a Christian one, not a Jewish one; specifically, I am looking at the way that Christians have used the exodus story to justify colonization. Because of this, for me and many Indigenous People around the world, this story is viewed as the basis for genocide. I invite you to hear an Indigenous perspective on this story.

It all starts out so well. The Israelites have been brought out of slavery by God, led by Moses. In Deuteronomy 5:1-6, we read:

> Moses called out to all Israel, saying to them: "Israel! Listen to the regulations and the case laws that I'm recounting in your hearing right now. Learn them and carefully do them. The LORD our God made a covenant with us at Mount Horeb. The LORD didn't make this covenant with our ancestors but with us—all of us who are here and alive right now. The LORD spoke with you face-to-face on the mountain from the very fire itself. At that time, I was standing between the LORD and you, declaring to you the LORD's word, because you were terrified of the fire and didn't go up on the mountain."
>
> The LORD said:
>
> I am the LORD your God, who brought you out of Egypt, out of the house of slavery.

God then gives the Ten Commandments to the people. This is the moral code of a people, set down as God's word, among them: "Do not kill" (commandment 6); "Do not steal" (commandment 8); "Do not crave your neighbor's house, field, male or female servant, ox, donkey, or anything else that belongs to your neighbor" (commandment 10).

Deuteronomy 6:4-9, one chapter later, reads:

Israel, listen! Our God is the LORD! Only the LORD!

Love the LORD your God with all your heart, all your being, and all your strength. These words that I am commanding you today must always be on your minds. Recite them to your children. Talk about them when you are sitting around your house and when you are out and about, when you are lying down and when you are getting up. Tie them on your hand as a sign. They should be on your forehead as a symbol. Write them on your house's doorframes and on your city's gates.

Again: What's not to affirm? But then we get to Deuteronomy 6:10-12:

Now once the LORD your God has brought you into the land that he swore to your ancestors, to Abraham, Isaac, and Jacob, to give to you—a land that will be full of large and wonderful towns that you didn't build, houses stocked with all kinds of goods that you didn't stock, cisterns that you didn't make, vineyards and olive trees that you didn't plant—and you eat and get stuffed, watch yourself! Don't forget the LORD, who brought you out of Egypt, out of the house of slavery.

Here's where I start having problems. Because in my cosmology as a woman indigenous to North America, I am one of *them* invaded by the people presumed to be chosen of God.

I am from the people who built the cities of clay on the crest of cliffs, mesas, that were seized by the Spanish; the people who originally lived in homes with good things in the river valley of what is now called the Rio Grande; the people who dug the wells in the desert that have been used and depleted by others for more than five hundred years; the people who planted the fields of corn and tobacco, the vines of squash and beans, the first people who were satisfied by these four sacred plants.

It is hard for me to relate to the protagonists in the Deuteronomic story, the colonizing force encouraged to destroy Native inhabitants—me and my people—totally. This is what Deuteronomy 7 says in verses 2-5:

> Once the LORD your God lays them before you, you must strike them down, placing them under the ban. Don't make any covenants with them, and don't be merciful to them. Don't intermarry with them. Don't give your daughter to one of their sons to marry, and don't take one of their daughters to marry your son, because they will turn your child away from following me so that they end up serving other gods. That will make the LORD's anger burn against you, and he will quickly annihilate you.
>
> Instead, this is what you must do with these nations: rip down their altars, smash their sacred stones, cut down their sacred poles, and burn their idols.

The Ten Commandments are clear in Deuteronomy 6: Do not kill. Do not steal. Do not covet. But in chapter 7, a handful of verses later, the germ of genocide is justified.

Deuteronomy became a core scriptural basis of the Doctrine of Discovery.

The new chosen people in a new promised land

An important premise of the Doctrine of Discovery goes like this: God made a covenant with Israel, God's chosen people. With the coming of Jesus, God's chosen became the church, the body of Christ. The church thus becomes the new chosen people who have a covenant with God, and who are justified and empowered to go into the promised land—that is, lands around the globe that were uninhabited by a Christian prince. As mentioned in chapter 1, this is the basis of the papal bulls that formed the foundation of the Doctrine of Discovery, the worldview of domination.

That worldview of domination was reinforced only once it hit the shores of what we now call the United States. In *Pagans in the Promised Land: Decoding the Christian Doctrine of Discovery*, Steven T. Newcomb explains how this paradigm or mental model of the "chosen people–promised land" story forms the imaginative foundation for the implementation of the Doctrine of Discovery in the United States, a foundation largely invisible to the people and culture that live within this worldview.[1]

The idea that America was a "chosen nation" called to a special destiny by God was part of the idea of the United States from the beginning. The New England Puritans in particular believed themselves to be the new chosen people entering the new promised land. As Donald M. Scott, professor of history at Queens College and the Graduate Center of the City University of New York, writes:

> John Winthrop, Governor of the Massachusetts Bay Colony, gave the clearest and most far-reaching statement of the idea that God had charged the English settlers in New

England with a special and unique Providential mission. "On Boarde the Arrabella, on the Attlantick Ocean, Anno 1630," Winthrop delivered the blueprint for what Perry Miller has dubbed an "errand into the wilderness" which set the framework for most of the later versions of the idea that "America had been providentially chosen for a special destiny." Winthrop delivered his lay sermon just before he and his fellow passengers disembarked on the shore of Boston harbor, the place, Winthrop proposed, to which God had called them to build up a model Bible commonwealth for Protestants in England and elsewhere to emulate. "Thus stands the cause between God and us. We are entered into Covenant with him for this work, we have taken out a commission," he declared, adding "if the Lord shall please to hear us and bring us in peace to the place we desire, then hath he ratified this Covenant and sealed our Commission and will expect a strict performance of the Articles contained in it."[2]

Genocide and the good news

This endorsement of genocide and domination is a hard message, I know. How do I square this message, this ongoing story, with the good news of the gospel?

In Luke 4, Jesus, who aligned himself with his Jewish prophetic tradition, speaks his mandate from the prophet Isaiah:

The Spirit of the Lord is upon me,
    because the Lord has anointed me.
He has sent me to preach good news to the poor,
    to proclaim release to the prisoners
    and recovery of sight to the blind,
    to liberate the oppressed,
    and to proclaim the year of the Lord's favor. (vv. 18-19)

As an Indigenous Christian, there is a lot to square between Jesus' mandate from Luke 4 and the text of Deuteronomy. George Tinker, author of *American Indian Liberation: A Theology of Sovereignty*,[3] offers me a way out of the conundrum. Tinker suggests that each People is entitled to bring its own old testament (the stories of its own people) to the mandate of Jesus. Tinker says we should not be made to interpret and reinterpret the history of one people we may have trouble relating to in geography and tradition. He asks each of us Peoples of earth to imagine what the gospel of Christ means in the context of our own "old testament."

Tinker argues that "the Creator's promises to each of our tribes, invested in our traditional stories and traditional ceremonies, are still valid and still a source of life and liberation for Native American Peoples. We need to find the courage and the strength to insist as whole communities that our traditional perspectives of and experiences of the Sacred are just as valid as the perspectives of the colonial Christianity imposed on our ancestors and enforced to this day."[4]

Tinker offers me an opportunity to claim the humanity of my people outside the narrative of the Old Testament by holding up the history of my own people alongside the life, message, and mandate of Jesus.

I admit that this discussion of the exodus story is discouraging. For me, as an Indigenous follower of Jesus, I have to leave it behind and embrace my own "old testament" in order to claim my faith. I would like to share a message of hope based on shared values. But this can feel hard for me to do. I have been walking in the shadow of the Doctrine of Discovery ever since I was called to write the "Statement on the Doctrine of Discovery and Its Enduring Impact on Indigenous Peoples"[5] on behalf of the World Council of Churches in 2011. I feel I must throw justified genocide into the fire if I am to walk with Jesus and strive to abide by his mandate.

Over the years, many people have argued that the papal bulls that formed the foundation of the Doctrine were a distortion of the gospel—a twisting of God's Word to justify empire-building. My careful read of the exodus story complicates this notion. While the commandments in Deuteronomy 5 make clear the wrongness of murder and theft, chapters 6 and 7 make a clear justification and program for genocide.

Some theologians argue that the supposed genocide of Canaanites never took place historically. But regardless, in his essay "A Native American Perspective: Canaanites, Cowboys, and Indians," Robert Warrior argues that the seventeenth-century Puritans' use of the exodus story empowered the murder of Native American people in New England and gave birth to manifest destiny and American exceptionalism in the United States.[6] For Native Americans and Indigenous Peoples around the world, the exodus story is one in which we are the Canaanites, not the Israelites.

At a recent faith gathering, an Indigenous leader asked me, "How can you be an Indian and a Christian, after everything that has been done to us?" A good question, especially for a scholar of the doctrine that justified the eradication of my people and remains the economic and political justification for continuing to do so to this day.

I return to Christ's mandate in Luke 4. I am a Christian because I am compelled by the mandate and example of Jesus. I am a Christian because I love him. I cling to the hope he proclaims: good news for the poor; the release of prisoners; liberation for the oppressed.

Liberation for the oppressed.

Lust for security

What is the purpose of the lie of justified genocide? It runs counter to the very nature of Jesus' mandate. Justified genocide explains why the powerful are entitled to plenty—*because God has mandated it*—while the oppressed go without—*which is also God's will.* Justified genocide explains that the powerful have the *right* to cause suffering and death.

Our country's economic system is built on this assumption; justified genocide plus capitalism have resulted in manifest destiny and American exceptionalism, which describe the bounty of the earth as ours for the taking. Our economic system is built around giving some people more security than they need at the expense of others who have almost none. It is a system of injustice. It is time for the Christian church to throw this lie into the fire.

If we as Christians gave up the presumed rightness of justified genocide, how might our behavior as a body change? Would we continue to invest our money, our efforts to ensure our security, in systems of death?

Jesus and the prophets speak vehemently against these systems.

In Matthew 9:13, Jesus tells the leaders of the church: "Go and learn what this means: *I want mercy and not sacrifice.*" This seemingly enigmatic statement requires more investigation. Jesus is quoting the prophet Hosea. Hosea 6:6 tells us what Jesus is referring to:

> I desire faithful love and not sacrifice,
>   the knowledge of God instead of entirely burned
> offerings.

In other words, the tithe God asks for is not symbolic, like burnt offerings, but concrete: mercy. Acknowledgment of God's plan as explained by the prophets: justice.

This theme come up again and again throughout the Prophets of the Hebrew Scriptures. Isaiah 1 says this:

> What should I think about all your sacrifices?
>   says the LORD.
> I'm fed up with entirely burned offerings of rams
>   and the fat of well-fed beasts.
>   I don't want the blood of bulls, lambs, and goats.
> When you come to appear before me,
>   who asked this from you,
>   this trampling of my temple's courts?
> Stop bringing worthless offerings. . . .
> Your hands are stained with blood.
>   Wash! Be clean!
> Remove your ugly deeds from my sight.
>   Put an end to such evil;
>   learn to do good.
> Seek justice:
>   help the oppressed;
>   defend the orphan;
>   plead for the widow. (vv. 11-13a, 15b-17)

Isaiah explains here that God's people are responsible for more than their individual sins—they are responsible for *structural* evil. Regardless of individual good deeds, the entire society Isaiah refers to is based on oppression. Laws, policies, practices are based on the strong profiting from the weak and the vulnerable—a society where the strength of the powerful comes from oppression.

In Amos 5, Amos describes the same society, a society that oppresses the weak at a structural level:

Truly, because you crush the weak,
    and because you tax their grain,
    you have built houses of carved stone,
    but you won't live in them;
you have planted pleasant vineyards,
    but you won't drink their wine.
I know how many are your crimes,
    and how numerous are your sins—
  afflicting the righteous,
    taking money on the side,
    turning away the poor who seek help.
Therefore, the one who is wise will keep silent in that time;
  it is an evil time.
Seek good and not evil,
    that you may live;
    and so the LORD, the God of heavenly forces,
    will be with you just as you have said.
Hate evil, love good,
    and establish justice at the city gate. (vv. 11-15a)

Do we replicate the same society described by Isaiah and Amos in our efforts to ensure our own security? I would say yes.

What do we sacrifice on the altar of our security?

Our society has collectively invested in a death machine—linear, reductive, destructive; a machine that destroys air, water, soils, the life-support systems upon which all of creation depends. And what does this death machine give us? Profit. Money that provides us short-term luxury, short-term security.

Luxury is not a word many Christians tend to relate to. We say to ourselves and to each other, that's not us! We do not exhibit lust for luxury! But our lust for security is manifest in our willingness to participate in systems of death to achieve what we perceive as security.

Many argue that the story of colonization happened long ago, but is over now. Although what happened in the past is regrettable, they say, things are as they are today. But the vulnerable continue to suffer from unjust systems created by the powerful that church institutions continue to profit from. We enjoy the benefits of private property gained through violence, and the wealth our property has provided us. We continue to invest our institutional retirement funds in extractive industries that destroy the life-support systems of the earth and prey on the weak. We benefit from the unjust policies of the systems we helped create. It is time for us to repent, to turn back.

All my relations

From an Indigenous perspective, the way Christianity is typically practiced is very human-centric. Stan McKay taught me the term *transversal*: if we are to survive and thrive, we must behave as though all of those around us are relatives. A transversal worldview is an understanding that you are "all my relations."

"All are sacred," Stan told me, "whether or not any are good."

When Christians behave as though we can own creation, we are breaking more than just a compact with humanity—we are breaking a compact with ecosystems that support all life. This includes water, soils, air, and animals. Believing you are separate from these things is actually a commitment to systems of death. Just as with a canary in a mine, the death of soil and animals is an indication that death for people is imminent. I think that every People group knew this at one time. This is not just a logic specific to Indigenous Peoples. It is a logic specific to all life, including humans, of every variety. The idea that huge groups of humans can forget it in pursuit of financial security is very strange indeed.

How might we as the body of Christ experience transformation if we believed all that surrounds us are our relatives? How might we experience transformation if we accepted the kinship offered to us by the worldview of Indigenous Peoples?

An Indigenous vision of mission is for justice and restoration for all of creation, including all people. Most Indigenous spirituality, Stan told me, does not have a scripture or a focus on a historical person; it is centered on the soil or creation itself. God cannot be understood without the land—God comes out of the soil—nurturing and sustaining us.

Wati Longchar, a Naga elder and theologian from India, described to me an Indigenous people of India who celebrate twenty-three festivals related to the soil. One name of God is Li-jaba (soil-real) and another is Li-zaba (soil-enter). One who enters the soil with the seed. Without the land, God ceases to work. We co-parent with the earth. "Humans are made of soil and breath," Wati told me.

As I mentioned in the previous chapter, Stan encouraged me to seek healing by returning to the land of my grandmother, this woman I never met, my ancestor. As I struggled to untangle how to confront the Doctrine of Discovery, I felt shadowed by anger and shame. I was coming face-to-face with the hurt and humiliation that had defined my young adulthood. I turned to Stan for wise counsel.

He explained a pathway toward healing for me: to seek the healing waters of my homeland. When he spoke these words to me, I knew they were true. But I didn't know how to go about it. I called my friend and mentor Mark MacDonald, who was at that time the National Indigenous Anglican Bishop for the Anglican Church of Canada. I explained that I had never lived on the land of my grandmother. "I feel ridiculous," I told Mark. "I don't know what to do, or where to start." Mark listened to me voice my anxiety: that my ignorance would exclude me from receiving meaningful connection with the land, that I would arrive with foolish hope, but leave humiliated and empty.

Mark had been the assistant bishop of Navajoland Area Mission. He voiced a love for the desert that defines my internal sense of home; the dark blue sky against red earth, the seemingly endless horizon. He had a suggestion for who might be willing to guide me. He introduced me to Steve Darden, a Diné elder who would become my dear friend and mentor. I flew with Dan and our son, Micah, to New Mexico, where I met Steve for the first time.

Steve instructed me to enter the water and pray for my grandmother. "Pray for the young woman who lost her son," he encouraged me. As I had told him, my father was taken at birth from his mother, my grandmother, and placed into a Catholic boys' home.

Steve guided me through this process as I returned to my ancestral homeland in northern New Mexico, walking on the soil where my grandmother walked. Connecting to this woman, my grandmother, through the soil, our mother. The soil itself was a source of healing for me. I left northern New Mexico renewed. In the water, I found connection with the ones who came before me, unblocking the connection between us through prayer.

Tore Johnsen,[7] a Sami reverend from Norway, argues in his essay "Listen to the Voice of Nature" that "Christian theology needs to move from an anthropocentric to an ecological paradigm, drawing upon important perspectives from Indigenous Peoples. We need to start to understand and experience ourselves as taken from the earth and woven into the great web of life. . . . The earth becomes part of our identity."[8]

I met Tore Johnsen in 2012 while campaigning for the Indigenous Peoples' program at the World Council of Churches. While at the United Nations Permanent Forum on Indigenous Issues that year, we were both invited to an Indigenous consultation at the church center across the street from the UN campus. Tore sang a *yoik*, or traditional Sami composition, to the roughly one dozen of us who met with the WCC that day. The yoik was like nothing I had ever heard before, as though I experienced something with a sense I didn't know I had: a sense of God. Lightning flashed every few seconds, thunder a half second behind. It felt as though the yoik initiated the storm. It came quickly and was gone.

This is how Ursula Länsman, Finnish musician, defines the yoik:

> A *yoik* is not merely a description; it attempts to capture its subject in its entirety: it's like a holographic, multi-dimensional living image, a replica, not just a flat photograph or simple visual memory. It is not *about* something, it *is* that something. It does not begin and it does not end. A *yoik* does not need to have words—its narrative is in its power, it can tell a life story in song. The singer can tell the story through words, melody, rhythm, expressions or gestures.[9]

Tore told us that a yoik traditionally honors a person, or an element of nature.

Tore explained that historically, the yoik was banned by the church, and was even made illegal in Norway. I am sure that this amazing creative power, this spirit song, could not go out of existence, because it is obvious to me that it is a gift given by the Creator to the Sami people. If not one yoik rang out for five hundred years, a child in the future would find the notes, the tone, would sing out a yoik without knowing its name. This is what I said to Tore that day in 2012. I felt I could sense the history of Tore's people, the way I experienced the history of my own people in the water in New Mexico.

Indigenous spirituality has been dismissed for centuries as idolatry. As a result, international mission initiatives have focused on either partnering with Christians or seeking the conversion of non-Christian populations. Wati Longchar told me, "Missionaries are the vanguard of extraction—they bring in schools and hospitals to land with resource deposits, [and] then drive out the Indigenous Peoples."

Is this Jesus' call to the church? To struggle in solidarity only with Christians or, worse, to fellowship with people internationally when our only intention is to convert/colonize? Mennonite scholar Walter Sawatsky makes this claim when he argues that God's mission is to "save" the three billion non-Christians in the world.[10] I advocate for a larger vision of mission, one which includes restoration for the whole of creation.

Those of us who live in the West by the accident of our birth have the opportunity to make amends, not symbolically but *actually*. As Westerners, we can acknowledge that we are on the hook to live justly. As the beneficiaries of injustice, we must resolve to dismantle the systems that perpetuate it. These systems

include the whole economic development apparatus that results in decades of debt for developing nations, and in displacement, disability, and death for the peoples of indebted nations,
especially for vulnerable communities. My people are suffering
at the hands of the mighty who remove us from our homes and
lifeways, separate our families, militarize our communities and
steal our traditional lands, extract fossil fuels, minerals, timber, and other wealth, leaving behind environmental destruction that pollutes our bodies and those of our descendants for
dozens of generations. If Christendom's vision of God's mission for the world is to convert three billion non-Christians to
Christianity, as Sawatsky claims, then the Christian church is
just as apostate as he denies that it is. If the focus of mission is
not seeking justice in solidarity with the vulnerable, then I have
no energy for it.

We must reimagine our theology together, and give up the
notion that the position of privilege in which we find ourselves,
a position of dominance over the oppressed, is justified by God.
We must renounce our claim that the genocide of the vulnerable was justified, and systems of oppression are ordained. We
must give up the notion that security in material wealth is even
possible.

Choose life; defend the oppressed

The nature of God, God's eternal nature and divine power, is
clear. Our instructions are clear. We must choose the systems of
Life over the systems of death: Defend the oppressed.

And we need not be afraid.

Despite the current political reality that surrounds us, we
can't be deceived that we are somehow in a battle with those we
perceive to be our enemies. There is only one side, and that is

the side of creation. There is only one reality, and it is defined by the principles of life.

Imagine a movement or a system that demands that adherents not breathe oxygen. A leader making this case need not be accused of being "wrong" or "corrupt," but simply doomed. He and his followers cannot live for more than a few moments! Not because of ideological notions or wickedness, but simply because they do not comply with the simplest principle of life, of reality. Anything that runs counter to these principles is doomed to fail.

Our mutual dependence, in the community of creation, is revealed. Slowly at first, one by one and in twos, we come together, converge. We are made to do this. Instructions are in the very fabric of our DNA: We must choose life. The systems of death seem eternal, universal. But they are flimsy—hollow. They do not conform to the logic of life, and therefore they will pass away, as all things must that tend toward death. This is our choice: to cooperate with the systems of life, with the Great Animator, or to choose to support the systems of death. There is a hard cost associated with this choice. To choose life means giving up the financial return provided by extractive industry. But the benefit is joining in the awesome project of creation, together with the Creator.

It is human to breathe the air, to dwell in the land, to need water and nourishment. All of us will tend toward systems that enable these things, ultimately. It is human to work together, to possess dignity, to speak and to be heard. It is human to be touched, to be loved, to feel sympathy, comradery, to experience forgiveness and compassion. Our fragile bodies require that we cooperate to survive, and these tools are ours by birthright. All of us are drawn to systems that enable these things.

Those we may call adversaries of life are not to be hated, but pitied. They are fools. The way of life cannot be thwarted; it is the only reality for us all. Because we do not see their failure in our lifespan is no reason to despair. The great unknown unfolds itself over millennia, across an ever-expanding universe. Those who seem mighty seem so only from a fleeting viewpoint—your presence, the truth that runs through your veins, through the ancient chain of your ancestors, bears testament to this truth. Do not be afraid. The ever-unfolding process of life, the Spirit of Life, the Creator, is a power with no end, and cannot be overcome.

SEVEN

Follow the Money

SURINAME IS RICH in gold, bauxite, and other precious minerals. Because of these resources, the land in the interior rainforest region—the traditional lands of Indigenous Peoples—has been divided into concessions[1] and allocated by economic development projects. While this is not what you will read on Suriname's Wikipedia page, I have been in discussion with financial and political leaders who have admitted that 100 percent of Indigenous lands have been given to concessions. Although many Indigenous Peoples continue to live on their traditional lands, their lands and resources are controlled by those powerful enough to buy concessions, such as developers and mining corporations, thanks to the continuing impacts of the Doctrine of Discovery.

Alluvial gold mining in the rainforest uses mercury to remove gold from sediments in and near rivers and streams. In Suriname, an estimated sixty tons of mercury are expelled into the environment each year by gold mining operations.[2]

Indigenous People, like the Wayana, often live along these contaminated waterways and depend on them for fish, their main source of protein. Of course, this mercury ends up in their bodies. In the village of Apetina, every person tested exhibits serious mercury contamination far in excess of international standards. Even if gold mining ceased today, the environment would be contaminated with mercury for many generations to come.

The toxic effects of mercury on human health have been well known and documented for more than forty years. Termed "Minamata disease" for the city in Japan where major industrial waste pollution poisoned in excess of forty thousand people, mercury poisoning is known for causing neurological damage, especially during prenatal development and via nutrition received during early infancy. There is no treatment for this "disease"—prevention is the only effective intervention.[3]

The "mercury problem" in Suriname has been documented since the beginning of the gold rush that began in the early 1980s. Public health researchers monitor this release of poisons into the environment, but do not treat the people affected by it. They only study them. Can you imagine studying but not treating pregnant women and newborn children exposed to mercury? This is comparable to the notorious Tuskegee Syphilis Study, where African American men who had contracted syphilis were neither informed of the infection nor treated, although they were monitored regularly by researchers who studied the progression of the disease.

As I have worked among communities in the Guiana Shield, where Suriname is located, I have seen up close the impact of mercury poisoning. In Apetina, I met a mother named Asterik who lost her baby daughter, Jolijn, to in utero nervous system damage caused by mercury. She buried her little daughter in the floor of her home in the village, under her hammock. She showed me Jolijn's grave when I visited her home. Since the Wayana people do not have title to their lands, which are controlled by concession owners, Asterik's village can be forced to leave at any time, without regard for Jolijn's burial site.

Colonization continues

The Doctrine of Discovery is often discussed in the past tense. I hear people lament what has happened, explaining to themselves that it is sad that Native Americans were killed in the settlement of the United States and Canada, but there isn't much we can do about it now. Those who take the history to heart even talk with shame about the actions of their ancestors. What few recognize is that the processes of displacing Indigenous Peoples from their homelands so that the powerful can appropriate and settle Indigenous lands is happening *now*, all across the world. Laws based on the Doctrine of Discovery continue to be created, and the processes of colonization continue. Indigenous Peoples are still intentionally being poisoned, brutalized, and displaced for their land and natural resources.

I was shocked to learn this reality through my work in Suriname. I realized that what is happening there today is the exact process that unfolded in North America 150 years ago. While attending the United Nations Permanent Forum on Indigenous Issues and attending meetings held by the World Council of Churches, I also learned that what is happening in the Suriname rainforest is happening around the world. I was befriended by Indigenous Peoples in the Philippines, West Papua, Sweden, Norway, Mexico, Nicaragua, Bolivia, Peru, Australia, New Zealand, Greenland, and many other countries. All faced legal forced removal from their lands. All faced

major human rights abuses—in many cases including target-
ed violence and extrajudicial killings. In nearly every country,
extractive industry was legally polluting land, causing disease,
forcefully removing communities from their lands, and killing
innocent people.

How are such atrocities allowed to occur? And how are such
atrocities actually legal? In this chapter, I will outline the *legal*
processes of displacement and exploitation that are happening
in Suriname. Suriname is not a unique case, but one rather
small example of a global process making it impossible for
Indigenous Peoples to thrive, or even survive, on six continents.

A primer:
Economic development and international aid

Before I begin the story of my time in Suriname, however, we
need to talk about economic development and international aid
generally. Most people in wealthy nations see our participation
in the development of poorer countries as altruistic and even
generous. We believe that helping poorer countries "develop"
economically improves the lives of those who are on the receiving end. However, the truth is that powerful countries bring
strong self-interests to how the development of poorer nations
is structured and how we might benefit from it. Nations and
multilateral institutions providing aid are often interested in
extracting resources cheaply and efficiently from less developed
nations, and in ensuring their own security.

Countries receiving international development aid are not,
for the most part, receiving outright gifts of cash from other
countries anymore, as they did in the early twentieth century.
"Aid" is most often provided in the form of loans, and with
strings attached. In order to receive these loans, the country

borrowing money must often revise national policies, such as by dismantling or weakening environmental laws, labor laws, and other laws that the lender views as barriers to free trade. The loosening of regulations is seen as creating an environment that will be attractive to investors. The loans are frequently backed by collateral in the form of land and raw materials from the borrowing countries. For instance, Suriname once had good environmental protection and labor laws, but since receiving loans from the Inter-American Development Bank, these laws have been gutted.

Multilateral international and regional banks like the International Monetary Fund (IMF), the World Bank, the Inter-American Development Bank (IDB), and the African Development Bank (ADB) seek to create conditions for further investment in these countries by funding infrastructure like roads and electric power; overseeing political processes to loosen regulations and attract investors; and conducting surveys to identify raw resources, like precious metals and lumber. For instance, to make the investment required to establish a large-scale mine, there must be security or stability on the ground, a "flexible" environment where business can take place legally, and cooperation from the government. Private investors will then come into the country with investment dollars to buy mining concessions, export ore for processing and adding value, and then deliver value-added resources to the global market.

Development programs provide funding for infrastructure, like roads and electric power. This infrastructure makes it easier for investors to extract raw resources and get them to market. For example, if the country receiving aid has minerals as a raw resource, the ore will be exported on ships and refined somewhere else so that the countries making the investment benefit most from the ore's extraction. Rather than create products in-country, where processing would provide local jobs and stimulate the local economy, the raw resource is exported so that the country that "adds value" or turns it into a consumer product will earn the greater part of the profit. The true value of the extracted resource is based on its resale value once it becomes a consumer product, like jewelry in the case of gold or flooring in the case of lumber. If the resource being extracted is labor, then the investing agency will develop tax-free international zones, or free-trade zones, where workers can provide labor without having to comply with the labor laws of the country receiving "aid."

Development loans bring dollars into the country's economy. But while these loans may make some people's lives better in the short term, development programs often have a terrible impact on the environment and on Indigenous and vulnerable Peoples who live in "undeveloped" regions considered "empty," as described in chapter 1. It is often their land and the raw materials and resources within it that are offered as security against development loans. Moreover, development programs do not reduce poverty for the bottom 20 percent of the population in the country being aided. Instead, these programs benefit the top 80 percent of the population but diminish well-being and result in displacement, disease, and death for the most vulnerable, such as Indigenous Peoples.

How does this happen? Indigenous and vulnerable peoples often have no legal claim to the land they occupy, as I have explained. Their governments may care about their plight, but when the country is indebted and needs the land to secure additional loans, the rights of Indigenous Peoples to their land go unheard. The land becomes privatized for "development" and resource extraction. When mining companies pay for land concessions in Suriname, for instance, the needs of the Indigenous and tribal Peoples who inhabit the land are secondary to the needs of the mine.

When the government—or the banks—comes in and privatizes the land, the Indigenous Peoples are in exactly the same position that the Yakama were when their lands were privatized via the Allotment Act. They can't live off the land the same way they used to and are now thrust into the market economy. They are displaced. This creates a crisis for people in these communities, who are now truly impoverished and whose health status is reduced to unacceptable lows when measured in terms of death, disease, disability, and a burgeoning rate of suicide. The assimilation process inherent to economic development results in lowered life expectancy among affected communities.

Moreover, resource extraction itself poses a direct threat. Mining processes threaten the lives of communities who depend on the forest for their livelihood. Waters are contaminated with effluent, including heavy metals like mercury and toxins like cyanide. The food web is likewise negatively affected. The toxins carried in the bodies of the animals are transferred to the bodies of the people. Mercury, for example, bioaccumulates, which means it is amplified by each trophic level of the food chain that digests it. Mercury is methylated by the bacteria in a stream. This bacteria is absorbed by small fish, who are eaten by larger fish, who are ultimately eaten by people. By the time the mercury makes it into the bodies of Indigenous and tribal Peoples who depend on fish as their primary source of protein, the original mercury is biomagnified a million times. There are approximately six trophic levels in the food chain in Suriname. Each one magnifies mercury approximately tenfold (some levels more, others less). Over the six trophic levels, biomagnification results in one million times greater toxicity once it reaches the body of an in utero human fetus.

If this is the result of "development" aid, how do these economic development programs justify their claim that they reduce poverty? Here's how: they use per capita gross domestic product as the measurement. If you try to measure and calculate per capita gross domestic product for people living traditional lifestyles, it will be very low—largely because they are not part of the market economy. They are living off their land. They're hunting, fishing, gathering foods, using medicines found in the rainforest, using materials found in the rainforest to build housing. They are buying and selling with money to much less of an extent than folks who are fully in the market economy. They are not as likely to have jobs for which they are paid in money. All of this means that, on paper, their per capita gross domestic product appears very low. Moving people into a market economy increases the flow of money and thereby gross domestic product. Globalization that converts land and resources held in common by people living subsistence lifestyles into private ownership thus appears to reduce poverty *when measured in terms of per capita gross domestic product.*

The development agencies know this. They have mountains of data and internal reports that explain that development programs damage the most vulnerable people. They have determined that this is an acceptable cost of doing business. What results is a slow-moving crisis of death by attrition among marginalized communities living in extreme poverty.

The slow-moving death by attrition of marginalized communities in developing nations creates a fast-moving crisis on a global scale. The reason: physical security and political security go together. The health of vulnerable populations is a requisite for sustained human development and national security. Those who feel insecure about their survival needs have a fundamentally different outlook and political behavior from those who feel secure. The health crisis among vulnerable and marginalized people is the aftermath of economic development. At the same time, it is the cause of serious social and political problems. This is the link between economic development programs and violence. Addressing the health crisis as a factor that contributes to political unrest is an essential requirement not only for improving health and sustaining human development but also for enhancing national security.[4]

To make this global process clearer, let's take a closer look to the experience of Suriname.

A case study in colonization:
The Suriname Land Management Project (SLMP)[5]

Suriname was historically a Dutch colony, reaching independence in 1975. The Netherlands had claimed the right of first discovery, per the Doctrine of Discovery. When Suriname gained independence, this ownership flowed to the national government of Suriname. Indigenous People did not own title to their traditional lands under Dutch authority prior to 1975, and likewise did not own title to their traditional lands under Suriname authority after 1975.[6]

According to *The Indigenous World 2019*, "The legislative system of Suriname, based on colonial legislation, does not recognize indigenous or tribal peoples, and Suriname has no legislation governing indigenous peoples' land or other rights. This forms a major threat to the survival and well-being of indigenous and tribal peoples, particularly given the strong focus that is being placed on Suriname's many natural resources (including oil, bauxite, gold, water, forests and biodiversity)."[7] All land in the interior of Suriname is considered to be the property of the government (known as domain land).[8] Because the interior forest region inhabited by Indigenous Peoples was prohibitively difficult to access, the process of colonization was delayed until the 1980s, when a gold rush drew thousands of prospectors to the forest. Technological advances had made it cheaper and easier to venture into the forest for gold and timber. The race for wealth was on.

In 1982, the military government reformed the land tenure system to eliminate speculation, resisting the capitalist principle of private ownership.[9] The laws at that time gave Indigenous Peoples "entitlements" to their villages and agricultural plots, "as much as possible, unless there is a conflict with the general interest."[10] This legal structure was ambiguous at best. Indigenous Peoples wanted a more specific policy that spelled out how land could be utilized, as did the Inter-American Development Bank.

Meanwhile, Suriname found itself in a cycle of debt to development banks, especially to the IDB. Suriname's government had borrowed money to modernize its infrastructure in the coastal region, where most of the population resides, and its creditors were pressuring it to underwrite the debt with land. This posed a problem because land containing the most valuable resources was inhabited by Indigenous villages filled with individuals following a traditional lifestyle. While the national government owned the land rights of all public lands, per the Doctrine of Discovery, Suriname's legal system did not have clear guidance for how to address rights to occupancy by Indigenous and tribal inhabitants. The Inter-American

Development Bank claimed that it would not lend additional money to the government of Suriname until it "acknowledged" Indigenous land rights, putting pressure on Suriname to "resolve" land disputes with forest peoples. In other words, the IDB required new policy to ensure shareholders would have clear access to resources they planned to extract, under the guise of clarifying Indigenous land rights. The Suriname Land Management Project, or SLMP, would thus serve as the "final solution" to land disputes.

On February 23, 2006, the Inter-American Development Bank presented the Suriname Land Management Project to the government of Suriname. Through the SLMP, the Inter-American Development Bank essentially replaced historical land tenure systems in Indigenous and tribal areas with an "active market system for land."[11] An assumption underlying the newly developed, open land market system was that it would provide "equal" access to land to all market competitors; an assumption of capitalism is that anyone can buy or lease land at market rates. Since Indigenous and tribal Peoples in Suriname's rainforest are not recognized as having a legal claim to their traditional territories, and because they do not have the financial or social capital to compete with foreigners for title of their traditional lands, the SLMP resulted in the transfer of land to foreign investors and Inter-American Development Bank donors. Traditional land tenure systems based on principles of social organization and kinship relations were effectively eradicated in favor of a global market system—just as the Allotment Act did in the United States in the 1800s.

Why would a country like Suriname choose to participate in an arrangement where their national, resource-rich lands would end up in the hands of foreigners? As I mentioned before, multilateral development banks provide loans and low-interest subsidies on the condition that the developing country agree to remove "excess" government controls and promote market competition.[12] The aim of these programs is to achieve long-term or accelerated economic growth in poor countries by restructuring their economies and reducing "government intervention" (like labor laws and environmental protections).

Governments like Suriname's are then forced to open up their economies to foreign "direct" investment and reduce their role in the economy by privatizing basic services (like healthcare), as well as state-owned industries and nonmarket land and natural resources.

Developing countries like Suriname are encouraged to specialize in industries in which they have a comparative advantage to address their balance of payments. A balance of payments is a record of international transactions that balances the earnings on exports minus payments for imports. The structure of balance of payments is a reflection of the degree to which the Suriname economy relies on the outside world for goods and services it imports. Countries like Suriname that are rich in natural resources specialize in the extraction of those natural resources so they qualify for subsequent installments of what amounts to collateralized loans that are divided into segments marked by milestone payments. The extraction of natural resources thus becomes the booming sector.

In Suriname, mining is the largest income-generating segment of the economy. According to *Indigenous World 2019*, "The World Bank has embarked on the implementation of its renewed Country Strategy for Suriname, with the announcement of an intended 25 million dollar loan for support to private sector development, in particular extractive industries and agrobusiness."[13]

The government of Suriname faces the twin problems of capital shortages and high fiscal debts. These problems result from an attempt to modernize infrastructure, and from financial realities left by colonialism.[14] Suriname adopted policies designed to attract foreign investment. These structural adjustment policies created a trap of "modernizing" while leaving the institutional cost to Indigenous Peoples and the environment, including Indigenous Peoples displaced by economic expansion activities.

In a separate meeting that same day of February 23, 2006, a bank operations specialist told Dan and me, "The Suriname Land Management Project is a final solution that will settle all land disputes in Suriname, including Indigenous lands where gold and timber resources are concentrated." Essentially, the bank wrote the policy to make the new arrangement legal, drafted the specific laws, and forced the government to adopt it. "They aren't going to like it," the operations specialist told us, "but they will do it because they have to."

Effectively, a non-transparent, non-democratic entity—the Inter-American Development Bank—introduced policy to the Suriname Parliament, wrote the laws, and pushed through their adoption in an unwilling sovereign nation. This process has led to the wholesale contamination of Indigenous lands, communities, and bodies. Suicide, disease, and death are the predictable outcomes.

What causes this mess

Economic policies promoted by international agencies and triggered by international free trade agreements have resulted in large-scale development projects on Indigenous lands and territories worldwide. Multilateral banks provide structural adjustment loans to fund infrastructure necessary for resource extraction and export.

When I begin talking about the processes that lead to suffering for so many people, reasonable Americans often ask what the victims have done to bring this on themselves. This is a natural response when looking through an individualist lens, the dominant point of view in the United States. Our culture often assumes that if a person is suffering, it must be because she did something to bring it on herself. We all have similar opportunities, we are told. Success is a simple formula of intelligence and hard work.

For Indigenous Peoples in the Guiana Shield, the factors controlling health and well-being are socially and economically formed.[15] That is to say, the threats to human health are caused by policies that make it legal for the powerful to pollute Indigenous lands for profit. But solutions proposed by well-meaning individuals and organizations often do not take into account the whole system and structures that created the problems, and focus instead on the individual behaviors of those affected. Effective public policy and prevention should be directed not toward technical or behavioral solutions to health problems at the individual level, but rather toward breaking existing social, political, and policy barriers to minimizing disease, disability, and premature death.

That's a mouthful! Let me give an example.

As I mentioned, since the mid-1980s the mineral-rich rivers in the interior region of Suriname have attracted large numbers of gold miners. Many small-scale gold miners use mercury, which bonds, or "amalgamates," with the gold, to separate gold particles from the soil. This process is effective, simple, and cheap—and technically illegal in Suriname. However, large-scale mines that hold land concessions collect taxes from these small-scale miners for the privilege of mining the waters on corporate concessions. This allows corporate mines to benefit financially from both alluvial (illegal) and bedrock (legal) mining. The government does nothing to police mining on rivers, since as concession holders the corporate mines are expected to do this policing themselves.

Once an area of a river has been mined, the pools created during the mining process are abandoned. These pools contain heavy metals and toxic chemicals, including mercury. They also create the perfect environment for mosquitoes to reproduce.

The coastal area of Suriname has been effectively free of malaria since 1968.[16] However, Indigenous and tribal Peoples who live in the interior region have more recently been plagued by malaria, with over fifty-seven thousand documented cases between 2000 and 2015 in a region populated by an estimated fifty thousand people. The chief intervention strategy has been to train Indigenous and tribal Peoples to use treated mosquito nets. Focusing on individual-level behavior modification implies that individuals get sick because they either choose not to protect themselves or don't know how. The solution seems simple: train the people to use mosquito nets, and they will be safer.

In reality, mosquitoes that carry and transmit malaria are able to flourish in the pools of standing water left by alluvial gold mining; malaria flourishes unchecked in the regions where gold mining occurs. Mining itself is the cause, since it creates the conditions that enable the proliferation of mosquitoes that carry malaria.

Efforts to end malaria that focus on distributing mosquito nets to Indigenous and tribal communities may prevent individual families from contracting this parasite. But it also removes responsibility from the principalities and powers that legalized the pollution of Indigenous lands and the removal and even murder of Indigenous Peoples for profit. Addressing gold mining itself by bringing a halt to alluvial gold mining would eliminate the conditions (pools of stagnant water) in which mosquitoes can reproduce and flourish. Moving the locus of responsibility from individuals (who had nothing to do with creating the problem) to structures (laws and policies set by the collective) is much more efficient, logical, and just than asking those with the least power to change their behavior.

This example illustrates the propensity of the dominant culture to blame individuals, often the most vulnerable, for their own suffering. If Indigenous People are contracting malaria, we reason, they must not know to use treated mosquito nets. By extension, if Indigenous People are being poisoned, they must not know not to eat contaminated food. This effectively removes responsibility from the principalities and powers that legalize the pollution of Indigenous lands for profit.

Following the money

When Dan and I first began sixteen years ago to seek redress for our partners in Suriname who were poisoned by mercury from gold mining, our first step was to approach the United Nations Environment Programme to investigate and monitor what was happening in Suriname. Surely, this organization would have the mandate and the power to stop this contamination, we thought. And, we were successful in our advocacy to the United Nations Environment Programme! We convinced them to set up a program in Suriname. We thought we had solved the problem.

The truth was, nothing changed for our partners. They were still being poisoned; they were still being displaced from their lands. We came to realize that the United Nations Environment Programme didn't have the power to actually stop these things from happening. We needed to find the people creating the economic development policy for the country of Suriname.

It took a lot of sleuthing, but we figured out that policy was the Suriname Land Management Project, of which the Inter-American Development Bank was a major funder. We decided to petition the IDB and advocate on behalf of the Wayana. We formally petitioned the IDB Independent Consultation and Investigation Mechanism, claiming that the Wayana people were adversely affected by the SLMP. Our petition read, in part,

> As a consequence of these program activities, Wayana men are forced to look for alternative hunting grounds, far from where they used to hunt. The Wayana report that they cannot drink the water from the creeks and rivers because it is polluted. This pollution is caused by gold mining. Members of the Wayana communities, especially women, are often sexually molested. Women report they are now afraid to go to their fields where they grow crops to work. Generally speaking, the Wayana face the following threats: 1) Displacement; 2) Militarization of their Territories by Mining Interests; 3) Vulnerability to Natural Disasters; 4) Food Insecurity; 5) Contaminated Water; and 6) health effects (e.g., mercury intoxication) associated with dumping of mine waste, river sedimentation, and human waste generated by a large influx of miners.

The Inter-American Development Bank formally acknowledged to us that the Suriname Land Management Project was going to be destructive to Indigenous communities. However, we were told, the project had already been funded and input into the SLMP was now closed. Our petition arrived five days too late. Well, surely then the Inter-American Development Bank would take some responsibility for the destructive nature of the SLMP and offer some restitution or recompense for Indigenous communities being harmed? No. The Inter-American Development Bank assumed no liability.

If we wanted to speak into policies like the Suriname Land Management Project, we were told, then we needed to intervene as the policy was being written. But even if we had managed to intervene before the SLMP had been finalized, influencing the crafting of such policies is almost impossible, we found out. The Organization of American States, which is a governing body for the Western Hemisphere, founded the Inter-American Development Bank in 1959. The member states of the Organization of American States, which include every country in the Western Hemisphere, appoint people to the Inter-American Development Bank Board of Governors. This board meets regularly to craft economic development policies like the Suriname Land Management Project. Banks are also invited to these meetings, since they are going to fund the projects that are co-determined by the member states.

But these meetings where policy is crafted and funding decisions are made are basically closed to outsiders. That means communities impacted by these policies and decisions have no access to this decision-making body. This would be as if no citizen in the United States were allowed to know what goes on in Congress. All you would know is that laws are being made that directly impact your life, and yet you would have no knowledge or say about this. Supranational institutions like the

Inter-American Development Bank are non-transparent and non-democratic. These are the institutions responsible for policies that poison our partners, yet the Native people of Suriname have no access to these structures. Nor did we.

Learning this, we tried another tack within the Organization of American States. We went to the Inter-American Commission on Human Rights. Suriname Indigenous Health Fund petitioned the Inter-American Commission on Human Rights on behalf of the Wayana people, which I presented before the commission in March 2014, accompanied by Doug Hostetter (the then director of the Mennonite Central Committee's United Nations Office) and Mark MacDonald (the then National Indigenous Anglican Bishop for the Anglican Church of Canada). The problem, we learned, is that the Inter-American Commission on Human Rights could propose sanctions against Suriname for Indigenous human rights abuses, but those sanctions would have no teeth. They are not enforceable by any organization or institution. In fact, the Inter-American Development Bank itself has wonderful policy regarding the need to respect Indigenous and human rights in economic development projects (termed "Development with Identity"), but that policy is both (a) rarely followed, and (b) unenforceable. There are literally no consequences for economic development projects that violate Indigenous rights, neither for the banks that fund them nor the countries that implement them.

Once we learned this, we tried the United Nations Special Rapporteur on Indigenous Issues. Surely, there would be some enforcement possible here, thanks to the landmark United Nations Declaration on the Rights of Indigenous Peoples (UNDRIP), a product of almost twenty-five years of deliberation by UN member states and Indigenous groups. The United

Nations Declaration on the Rights of Indigenous Peoples was adopted by the UN in 2007 to enshrine rights that (according to Article 43) "constitute the minimum standards for the survival, dignity and well-being of the indigenous peoples of the world."[17] Clearly, the contamination of the bodies and lands of the Native Peoples of Suriname was counter to the United Nations Declaration on the Rights of Indigenous Peoples.

Again, we found out, the problem is that the United Nations Declaration on the Rights of Indigenous Peoples—like the Paris Agreement to combat climate change—is a voluntary agreement. If a UN member state (or Paris Agreement signatory) violates the policy, there is no penalty for such a violation, no way to hold the violator accountable. What we learned is that the UN is a largely symbolic body—a platform for diplomacy. It is not possible for them to truly hold accountable a country committing human rights abuses. We petitioned other international bodies like the World Health Organization, hoping they could do this. They could not.

What we came to realize is this: If a company is leaching mercury into a river that an Indigenous community depends on for food and water, and supranational structures have agreed that it is okay to do this and have made it legal, then tough luck. In fact, the situation is far more severe than even this pollution. Through economic development policies, Indigenous Peoples had been stripped of their lifeway, economy, homes, and communities. Even families had been divided, as any child seeking an education beyond the fifth grade must attend boarding school in the coastal region hundreds of miles from their parents, communities, language, and culture. Our own U.S. understanding of eminent domain demands at least compensation for lost resources. Weren't the forces who had taken so much from our partners obligated to provide access to alternative lifeways, economies, homes, and communities?

When we followed the money, we found out the answer: No.[18]

I want to say here that our inability to effect meaningful structural change does not mean that structural change cannot be brought about. But for structural change to occur, it is going to take collective action. While the systems of death may be able to dismiss Dan's and my attempts at reform, the body of Christ might not be as easily dismissed.

Individual sin and structural evil

The inclination to focus on individual solutions to systemic problems is a natural response when looking through an individualist lens, the dominant point of view in the United States. If a person is suffering, as a culture we often assume it is because she did something to bring it on herself. Similarly, when Christianity is understood through an individualist worldview, emphasis falls on sins committed by individuals, and personal piety and individual conversion are seen as the means to salvation.

However, the Bible asserts that God's people are responsible for more than their individual sins—they are responsible for *structural* evil. Throughout the Prophets and the prophetic teachings of Jesus, the people are called to resist systemic injustice and oppressive laws that exploit those in need to benefit the powerful.

I return again to Amos, who describes a society that oppresses the weak at a structural level:

Truly, because you crush the weak,
    and because you tax their grain,

you have built houses of carved stone,
     but you won't live in them;
you have planted pleasant vineyards,
     but you won't drink their wine.
I know how many are your crimes,
     and how numerous are your sins—
afflicting the righteous,
     taking money on the side,
     turning away the poor who seek help.
Therefore, the one who is wise will keep silent in that time;
     it is an evil time.
Seek good and not evil,
     that you may live;
and so the LORD, the God of heavenly forces,
     will be with you just as you have said.
Hate evil, love good,
     and establish justice at the city gate. (Amos 5:11-15a)

Regardless of individual good deeds, the entire society Amos refers to is rooted in oppression. Laws, policies, and practices are based on the strong profiting from the weak and the vulnerable—a society where the strength of the powerful comes from oppression. Just as the small-scale, individualist approach of mosquito nets will not solve the problem of malaria in Suriname, neither will personal piety address the systemic and structural sins of resource extraction causing the oppression, objectification, and exploitation of other human beings.

Following the money back home again

You may be surprised, as I once was, to find out that colonization is current and ongoing, and that the global economic policy of domination and displacement of Indigenous Peoples is continuous and legal. These policies that dominate and displace operate globally, including in North America, as we see with the pipelines being built across the Midwest, and with coal, gas, and uranium mining on Indigenous lands. Around the world, Indigenous Peoples are being denied rights to their economies and their traditional hunting and fishing lands by the removal of environmental protection for the lands and waters they depend on for food and shelter—all in the name of "economic development." In the name of making money.

Kind and generous people often believe that we are just missing something—that our system is truly good and democratic, and that my analysis cannot possibly be true. Frankly, this is the perspective of the privileged who cannot imagine that systems that have long benefited them could cause so much damage to others.

And here's something else I came to realize: *This process of displacement and exploitation is not removed from congregations and parishioners that invite me to speak to them.*

Large-scale mining in Suriname—including that done by the Newmont Corporation, a mining company based in Colorado—is responsible for the destruction of not just one people but many. Mining destroys the river systems that thread through the Amazonian region, displacing traditional societies, like the Wayana, who depend on the river for their livelihood. Mining zones are militarized, and communities are displaced, harassed, and even killed for the ore that lies below their traditional lands. Communities are destroyed. Lives are destroyed. For money.

Mining processes load the environment with mercury and cyanide. A major mine in negotiation with the Matawai people has in my presence admitted to discharging huge quantities of cyanide into the river system multiple times each year. What was once considered a global disaster has now become a routine event in Suriname. The nervous systems of Indigenous adults and children who live in the region are ravaged by mercury, a toxin they are exposed to throughout their lives, beginning when they are forming in the womb.

While the mining industry is both wealthy and powerful, the government of Suriname receives a relatively small portion of the profits from concession holders. Trade deals are negotiated with the help of multilateral governance structures, where heads of state work through institutions like the Organization of American States and the Group of Twenty, or G20, to make deals. The rules of trade are arranged to benefit the developed world so that we can say, "See, we paid for the right to extract resources from this country! We do it legally!" In reality, this means polluting the country. We, the developed world. Committing structural evil just like Amos described.

Many denominations are invested in mineral extraction, and in oil. We individually and collectively are the beneficiaries. My own denomination, Mennonite Church USA, is invested in Newmont mining.

Everence is a Mennonite faith-based financial services organization. Members of the Dismantling the Doctrine of Discovery Coalition approached Everence to learn how we might work together to persuade the Newmont Corporation to acknowledge the human rights of the Indigenous Peoples living in mining-impacted regions. The coalition received an explanation from an Everence employee responsible for social screening that outlined how church investment through Everence is handled, which I paraphrase in the following paragraphs.

Buying Newmont shares is not a deliberate decision by Everence, but is part of an automatic process just following an index model in a passively managed fund. Not all mining or petroleum companies are accepted by Everence; there is an exclusionary list that tries to exclude the worst of the worst. Newmont is not on that exclusionary list. Newmont is in the middle range of mining companies in terms of their environmental and social justice activities, so it doesn't trip Everence's screening process.

Everence does not consider Newmont to be perfect, but given that Newmont has signed on to the Compact for Responsive and Responsible Leadership, the overall sentiment is that Newmont has made great strides in environmental responsibility. Meanwhile, Everence welcomes input from folks on the ground who are aware of the activities of various corporations. Investment in general is a gray area, meaning there are no "pure" investments. Anything followed to its roots—what is used, what we eat, how we travel—is always compromised along the way. Everence, being a fiduciary agent for investors, tries to be responsible, but operates in that realm of gray. In other words, if it were strictly an activist organization, it could not invest anywhere and would cease to exist.

I understand the allure, the desire for wealth and ease. It is not easy to give up financial security. I want the same things everyone wants: ease for my children, and the assurance that I will be able to pay for their college tuition; a safe and beautiful home; assurance that when I grow to be an elder, I will not be a burden on my children or on society. Further, I crave independence, and wealth can give that to me. I also want to feel the satisfaction of being wise and thrifty; I want the assurance that my good choices have entitled me to an ease that I have earned.

I want all of these things. But my ease and self-satisfaction are not worth the lives of my partners, and the millions of vulnerable people around the world who are sacrificed on the altar of security.

The Doctrine of Discovery and me . . . and you

Your retirement account very likely benefits directly from economic development loans. Multilateral development banks like the Inter-American Development Bank sell their economic development loans to private banks, who repackage them and then sell them to financial services companies like TIAA-CREF, Fidelity, and so on.

In addition, oil, natural gas, gold, and other precious metals provide the economic engine that drives the global economy. Your retirement and other investment accounts are likely invested in extractive industries—like Newmont Corporation—that are poisoning the bodies and lands of Indigenous Peoples. We directly benefit from the displacement and oppression of Indigenous Peoples. Today. Right now.

In 2014, a small band of Miskitu leaders of Nicaragua asked Dan and me to help them in the way we were attempting to help rainforest peoples in Suriname. They had heard my testimony at the Inter-American Commission on Human Rights, and felt we might be able to help them. They explained that we (Suriname Indigenous Health Fund) were the only Westerners they had heard of who work directly for Indigenous communities. We agreed because the crisis they face is urgent. The Miskitu are removed, disappeared, and killed simply for inhabiting land their government believes is economically valuable. For years, we received human rights testimony weekly, sometimes many times a week. This testimony was frequently accompanied by pictures of dead and wounded. There are lists of those who are dead, and disappeared. Many displaced families continue to live in the forest without adequate food, clean water, or medical aid. Extreme violence resulted. Displaced Miskitu people driven from the lands guaranteed them by treaty have taken up arms in bloody skirmishes with encroaching settlers empowered by the national government.

Peacemaking as it is commonly defined focuses on asking the vulnerable not to use violence to defend themselves and their families. Many churches, including my own in the peace tradition, want to ask victims of colonization to try to solve their conflicts with words and diplomacy rather than taking up arms. This is offensive. If we want Indigenous Peoples to live without violence, then *we* must actively dismantle the violence inherent in our economic structures. If peacemakers want to stop violence, we need to tear down the structures that cause death and disease, the war of attrition, that some Indigenous and vulnerable people oppose with force to save the very lives of their loved ones. To ask the most vulnerable not to engage in self-protection when we have the power to stop structural violence is, at the very least, hypocrisy.

As an institutional church, we have the opportunity to engage the structures in defining a pathway toward life. Cynthia Moe-Lobeda calls this resisting structural evil.[19] She argues, "While structural evil may be beyond the power of individuals to counter, it is composed of power arrangements and other factors that are humanly constructed and therefore may be dismantled by other decisions and collective actions."[20] Dan and I were not successful in our first attempts. But together with you and others, we might be.

We can engage directly with institutions, as Dan and I have done. But we can also demand and facilitate direct negotiation between Indigenous Peoples and their governments, international institutions, and extractive industry. This may be hard to imagine because processes like this don't yet exist. But the institutional church has the moral authority to act as arbitrator, and the economic clout to see it through. By doing this, we create the conditions where the world can acknowledge the ongoing violence, and *intervene* before armed conflict emerges. John Paul Lederach, musing about moral imagination that "transforms human affairs without violence," writes, "We need eyes that peer into the hidden mysteries below the visible realities."[21]

Does not the Great Animator, the Ancient of Days, the Spirit of Life, burn within us? Are we not salt, light? As Moe-Lobeda writes, "As 'I's' that are 'we's' spanning the globe, and as 'we's' attentive to the beckoning of God whose love will bring abundant life for all, we are replete with moral power. That divine love breathes in us, urging us to dedicate intelligence, creativity, energy, political savvy, skill, and the song of our souls toward a world in which all people and all of creation may flourish."[22]

Like the prophets, we can call systems of power to account, into negotiation and conciliation. We can choose to stand with the oppressed in a call for justice.

EIGHT

Solidarity and Repair

They seek me day after day,
    desiring knowledge of my ways
    like a nation that acted righteously,
    that didn't abandon their God.
They ask me for righteous judgments,
    wanting to be close to God.
"Why do we fast and you don't see;
    why afflict ourselves and you don't notice?"
Yet on your fast day you do whatever you want,
    and oppress all your workers.
You quarrel and brawl, and then you fast;
    you hit each other violently with your fists.
You shouldn't fast as you are doing today
    if you want to make your voice heard on high.
Is this the kind of fast I choose,
    a day of self-affliction,
    of bending one's head like a reed
    and of lying down in mourning clothing and ashes?

Is this what you call a fast,
    a day acceptable to the Lord?

Isn't this the fast I choose:
    releasing wicked restraints, untying the ropes of a yoke,
    setting free the mistreated,
    and breaking every yoke?
Isn't it sharing your bread with the hungry
    and bringing the homeless poor into your house,
    covering the naked when you see them,
    and not hiding from your own family?
Then your light will break out like the dawn,
    and you will be healed quickly.
Your own righteousness will walk before you,
    and the Lord's glory will be your rear guard.
Then you will call, and the Lord will answer;
    you will cry for help, and God will say, "I'm here."
If you remove the yoke from among you,
    the finger-pointing, the wicked speech;
    if you open your heart to the hungry,
    and provide abundantly for those who are afflicted,
    your light will shine in the darkness,
    and your gloom will be like the noon.
The Lord will guide you continually
    and provide for you, even in parched places.
    He will rescue your bones.
You will be like a watered garden,
    like a spring of water that won't run dry.
They will rebuild ancient ruins on your account;
    the foundations of generations past you will restore.
You will be called Mender of Broken Walls,
    Restorer of Livable Streets. (Isaiah 58:2-12)

This passage in Isaiah is important to me. I have included it because I would like you to read it for yourself. What is the prophet's message? What is God's call to action, voiced by the prophet?

I have rewritten it here, in words that relate to our own time.

These communities of privilege ask me for decisions they consider to be fair. They believe they are entitled to God's presence among them.

"We do good works, but you don't seem to notice," they tell me. "You just criticize us."

"We are good people; you can tell by our thrift and piety. Plus, we tithe. Most of what we tithe benefits our own community, but some small percentage we give in charity."

Your "good works" mainly benefit yourselves.

Your charity doesn't excuse you for participating in injustice. You exploit the workers in your society by benefiting unfairly from their labor. You feel entitled to cheap groceries even though large-scale agribusiness exploits immigrants in an arrangement that amounts to slavery; harsh chemicals they are forced to endure cause birth defects in their children, but they have no rights to healthcare.

You say your allegiance is to God but you invest your money in industries that destroy the earth and hurt vulnerable peoples: industries like oil and natural gas extraction, and mining. Your charity doesn't offset the way you are exploiting the most vulnerable among people; human trafficking, violence, and war are the result.

You can't act this way and expect God to listen to your prayers.

Do you think God considers your personal "sexual piety," tolerance toward your own friends, and the pittance you donate without getting involved good works? Does this feel like a sacrifice to you?

These are the good works that are acceptable to the Creator:

Loose the chains of injustice. Set the oppressed free and break every yoke of bondage and injustice. Share *your food* with the hungry. Eat with them, learn who they are, so that you find common cause with them. Demand rights for immigrants—make sure they have shelter, and their children are not taken from them and put into camps at the border. Make sure their needs are taken care of by struggling for just laws and policies. Stop turning away from your own flesh and blood—that is what the people you victimize are: *your relatives*. Your flesh and blood.

If you do these things the Creator has demanded of you, then you will be a light to the world, like Jesus. You will be healed.

The light of your identity in the world will go before you, and the Creator will back you up with the glory of creation.

Then when you call out to the Creator for help, the Creator will answer you right away! You will cry out for help, and the Creator will immediately respond! The Creator is not an abstract idea, the way you pretend. Your justifications for your bad behavior have created a false idea of God that is abstract and distant. But God is nearby! Because you are unjust, God simply doesn't listen to your prayers.

If you crush the yoke of oppression—if you quit pointing the finger at politicians, passing the buck, and rationalizing why it's not your job to intervene—if you give up your own security for the hungry and needy and satisfy the needs of the oppressed, then your light will fill up the darkness—the wicked nighttime of your age will be a brightness as full day.

The Creator will guide you always—that is the Creator's promise. The Creator will satisfy your needs in a land full of life, strengthening the earth, your bodies, and the bodies of your children.

You will repair ancient wrongs, and set things right. You will be known the world around as Restorers, menders of broken walls.

On May 25, 2020, George Floyd was accused of passing a counterfeit twenty-dollar bill to a cashier in Minneapolis. During his arrest, Floyd was killed by Derek Chauvin, a Minneapolis police officer who knelt on Floyd's neck for over eight minutes. George Floyd's death inspired national outrage, a final straw in a decades-long legacy of police brutality targeting African Americans, especially men. In Portland, Oregon, activists demonstrated publicly almost daily from May through October, drawing crowds each day numbering from hundreds to thousands. In July, the Trump administration deployed federal law enforcement agents to Portland to quell unrest. Federal agents in camouflage and tactical gear arrested dozens of demonstrators, packing them into unmarked vehicles.

Televised images of young demonstrators being detained by unidentified federal agents disturbed Bev Barnum, a self-described suburban mother. She felt she had to act.[1] She had never been involved in demonstrations before, but when she saw young protestors being treated in a way she considered "bullying" by federal agents, she got involved. She reached out to other women like herself, suburban mothers, by putting out a call on social media to join together in forming a "wall of moms" that would surround demonstrators. The group assembled with demonstrators wearing bright yellow "wall of moms" T-shirts. As a mother, Bev felt her role was to protect young people. So she put her body between law enforcement agents and the youthful demonstrators she felt were under attack.

By forming the wall of moms, Bev Barnum made a fundamental shift in her position. She and the women who joined her stepped across a line: from the sidelines, watching protests unfold on media from their homes, to the front lines, putting their bodies at risk along with demonstrators. While they might have felt sympathy for demonstrators while watching from the sidelines, the shift in position committed them to share the fate of demonstrators.

The wall of moms demonstrated true solidarity. The suburban mothers who originated the group were not relatives of George Floyd, were not African American, and were not the objects of unjust police attention, yet they chose to physically stand with the Black community in their demands for justice.

Solidarity is not symbolic. It is a conscious change in position, where those who are not threatened with oppression step across a line—from the sidelines to sharing the fate of the oppressed. When those who benefit from structural violence find they cannot tolerate the injustice any longer and join with those harmed by the systems of death, solidarity is the result.

I frequently hear people of faith use the word *solidarity* when they are talking about symbolic action. We signed a letter "in solidarity." We went to a meeting "in solidarity." But from the position of the oppressed, true solidarity is choosing to join with those under threat, by changing position.

Alan Paton, a white South African who devoted his life to dismantling apartheid in his own country, describes the process of changing position in his book *Cry the Beloved Country*.

I shall no longer ask myself if this or that is expedient, but only if it is right. I shall do this, not because I am noble or unselfish, but because life slips away, and because I need for the rest of my journey a star that will not play false to me, a compass that will not lie. I shall do this not because I am a hater of my own, but because I cannot find it in me to do anything else. I am lost when I balance this against that, I am lost when I ask if this is safe, I am lost when I ask if men will approve. Therefore, I shall try to do what is right, and to speak what is true.

I do this not because I am courageous or honest, but because it is the only way to end the conflict of my deepest soul. I do it because I am no longer able to aspire to the highest with one part of myself, and to deny it with another. I do not wish to live like that, I would rather die than live like that.[2]

You must do what you can't *not* do.

Symbolic solidarity: Our early attempts

In our work with Indigenous Peoples in Suriname, we began with symbolic solidarity. It was our attempt at true solidarity. This bore mixed results, which I describe below. Did our action yield what was wanted? Or did it make things worse by aligning powers against the powerless, and internalizing the knowledge among our partners that unstoppable forces are aligned against them?

Mercury from mining causes death, disease, disability, and suicide among Indigenous People in the Amazon. I have described this again and again in the pages of this book. In 2003, two years before Dan and I formally established Suriname Indigenous Health Fund, we adopted a policy on Indigenous People's rights that recognized the voice and life-knowledge of the Wayana people in the transborder region between Suriname and French Guiana. The Wayana do not participate in gold mining, and in fact live in an area upstream from where large-scale gold mining occurs. The physical location of their village, upstream of mining activities, is used by the government and also by scientists as evidence for why they are unaffected by gold mining. Yet their communities and bodies are devastated by mercury pollution discharged by gold mining. We viewed the Wayana's situation as a symbol of structural violence, where Indigenous health was sacrificed by economic development projects financed by international financial institutions like the Inter-American Development Bank.

According to our policy, *we would talk "with" Indigenous communities instead of talking "about" or "to" them.* The goal was for the victims to have a seat at the table. More specifically, we defined these goals: to humanize victims suffering exposure to mercury from mining and involuntary assimilation; to discourage support for economic policies based on self-interest; to encourage collectively envisioned policies based on humanism, life, and equality.

We were dedicated to a process of humanization. We wanted to turn the Wayana "situation," as it was passively described by public health researchers, into an actionable issue that required change. We were acting as social workers, connecting responsible people in government and industry with their victims, so that people in power could imagine themselves in the role of the victim. We assumed that if decision-makers understood what it felt like to be in the position of a Wayana, if they fully understood the consequences of their decisions, they would feel horrified at actions they had taken and change course. They didn't. We assumed the Wayana were resilient, and that if they had support, they would be the people best informed to cope with their situation, to find culturally relevant solutions and carry them out. We assumed the Wayana would be able to confront their aggressors with more credibility, passion, and firsthand knowledge than we could as outsiders. We assumed that supporting and empowering Indigenous communities would enhance their sense of dignity and pride and would counteract their stigmatization and isolation.

We began by providing portable, state-of-the-art equipment to Wayana communities so they could self-diagnose the effect of mercury on their community's health. Together with community leaders, we collaboratively defined research objectives and culturally appropriate methods. While "legitimate" researchers had been collecting data concerning impacts of mercury on Wayana communities for decades, results had not been shared with community members. In fact, the national government argued that since there is no treatment or cure for mercury poisoning, it is inappropriate to inform affected individuals of their condition. We disagreed with this, believing that it is a fundamental right of every patient to be informed when diagnosed with disease. The Wayana communities we worked with voiced frustration that they had been kept in the dark about their own health, when they could see the obvious symptoms of sickness all around them.

Our methods were rejected by economists and opposed by international health practitioners, who felt that only public health experts could appropriately engage in this level of research. In correspondence, they described community members as "neolithic" and "stone-aged."

Regardless of this assessment, self-diagnosis studies were successful. Community members collected their own data, participated with us in data analysis, and led data interpretation. Appropriate interventions were identified by the communities themselves, not outside experts. After this initial success empowering Indigenous communities to self-diagnose the effects of mercury on their community's health, however, victim-led advocacy had an unintended disempowering effect. Our efforts inadvertently gave government forces the opportunity to align themselves in opposition to the Wayana, and to prove again to the Indigenous communities advocating for health, human rights, and social justice—and to foreign supporters like us—that we are subordinate to state interests. We were left wondering if our approach had, in fact, had a disempowering effect on Indigenous communities by forcing an oppressed and occupied people to confront their oppressor and be reminded of their subordinate role.

We were able to publish studies demonstrating the impact of mercury on Indigenous communities, and ultimately bring about government acknowledgment that harm was occurring, though the government had previously denied it. We were able to initiate outside intervention. Our work prompted the United Nations Environment Programme to set up shop in Suriname. However, little has effectively changed for the affected communities. The Wayana engaged in the difficult work of proving their case all the way to the Organization of American States Inter-American Commission on Human Rights in 2014, but at the community level, little has changed.

When our efforts of a decade failed to empower the powerless to change their own fate, we were forced to recognize that, despite our best intentions, we are not seen as standing with Indigenous communities in solidarity but instead are privileged members of the group responsible for their colonization and alienation. Our society benefits from the gold mining that endangers their communities, culture, health, and very lives. As noted earlier, the national church of which we are members is even an investor in Newmont Corporation, a primary mining interest in Suriname. While we may be able to come and "help," we can always return to our homes and lives in the relative safety of the wealthiest, most powerful country on earth. Please don't misunderstand me to mean that we regret this work. In fact, this work continues. But in itself it is not enough; it amounts to charity. We must support the work of the Wayana where they are, in their own communities. But we must also move from a "helping" mode to a partnership mode.

Reflecting on our failure, we came to these questions: Should acting justly be something the powerful (us) should take personal responsibility for—confronting economic aggressors with our credibility, passion, and firsthand knowledge as people of privilege? Should challenging the economic powers, the principalities, powers, and rulers of darkness "in high places" (Ephesians 6:12 KJV) be primarily *our* concern, since these principalities and powers originate in our society?

We have come to the conclusion that the work to confront economic systems that benefit us and harm others must be our own. While we follow the leadership of our Indigenous partners as they identify the problems that need to be addressed in their own communities and form the solutions for how to address them, we accept responsibility for confronting and petitioning our own economic systems that cause death, disease, and disability to the vulnerable.

The Wayana are not the beneficiaries of the global systems that plot their demise. We are the beneficiaries. Their misery fuels the world's economic engine. The Wayana, along with hundreds and even thousands of Indigenous and vulnerable peoples across six continents, are sacrificed on the altar of extraction. It is those of us privileged enough to stand on the sidelines who must seek true solidarity by placing ourselves, our congregations, and our faith institutions between the systems of death and the vulnerable. This is a step beyond "bearing witness," beyond "service delivery," beyond "symbolic solidarity."

A Dutch friend and fellow Mennonite sponsored a speaking tour for me through several European countries in 2012. He also accompanied me, introducing me to congregations and NGOs he felt might be able to help me organize ecumenical support for the movement that Indigenous faith-leaders and I hoped to bring to the World Council of Churches 10th Assembly in 2013. He had traveled to Suriname on a human rights delegation sponsored by SIHF, where he had connected with Indigenous leaders and heard their stories firsthand. One evening, while we sat in a Swiss café, he told me with kindness in his eyes, "We must write a requiem for the Wayana." A requiem is a mass for the souls of the dead. While I appreciated his kindness, I fiercely disagreed with this sentiment. It is not enough to witness and acknowledge the deaths of the vulnerable. We must resist their slaughter. We must object to the forces that would sacrifice their lives as fodder for the economic engine of death.

Systems of death

Resource extraction is the world's economic engine today. It is every bit as destructive to humanity as the economic engine of slavery was. Slavery created the blueprint for transcontinental genocide. The United States continues to be haunted by legal inequity, institutional discrimination, disparities in health, life

expectancy, and poverty, and an outcry for justice that continues to rock our society 150 years after the end of slavery.

Resource extraction as an economic engine is doing these
things as well, while further destroying humanity's ability to
dwell on the earth. Why do we consent to systems of death?
Why do we consent to environmental pollution and, indeed,
the destruction of all the life-support systems of the earth? Oil
pipelines and fracking endanger groundwater; coal and petroleum emissions form the basis of climate change; subsurface
and placer mining processes load soils and waters (atmosphere,
geosphere, and hydrosphere) with toxic chemicals, the impacts
of which go on for thousands of years, spanning geologic time
frames. I pose to you that we consent to this destruction out of
a lust for security.

It's not wrong to want security in our lives—to know that
our basic needs will be taken care of no matter our status in
life. The problem is that we live in a world in which, for many
people, the need for security has turned into the lust for security. We would all agree that it's natural to eat food when one is
hungry. But gluttony is a different thing altogether—it is the
inordinate desire to consume past the point where our hunger
is satiated. Like gluttony, our inordinate desire for security is so
strong that we will throw other people—and indeed our planet
—under the bus in order to satisfy it.

Our economic system is built around giving some people
more security than they need at the expense of others who
have almost none. It is a system of injustice. And Jesus and the
prophets speak vehemently against these systems.

Dan and I have fully divested from financial systems that
are connected with resource extraction. This is not a righteous
act, or an act worthy of praise. We have simply crossed the line,

positioning ourselves with the oppressed. We have voluntarily given up wealth and security afforded to us by trading in the stock market because we cannot stand to benefit from these systems. We have thus effectively made ourselves vulnerable.

We have called on mining corporations in Suriname and in French Guiana to negotiate directly with communities affected by mining. We have engaged in advocacy in the U.S. Congress and mobilized people of faith to demand that the U.S. Treasury comply with international human rights conventions in the administration of foreign aid. We have called on the Inter-American Commission of Human Rights to effect policy that will sanction the Inter-American Development Bank for violating its own policies on development with dignity. We have engaged with the United Nations Universal Periodic Review, which publishes the state of human rights for every member nation, and we have also contributed to UN shadow reports.[3] We have attempted to penetrate the many layers of the G7, striving to advocate to the powers that form international development policy agreements. These actions are not righteous acts or worthy of praise. We have simply waded into the conflict, positioning ourselves in front of the most vulnerable. *We do not ask for or expect the least resourced, most vulnerable people to do this work.* We are effectively attempting to hold back our own institutions.

This work is expensive. It is exhausting. It is frustrating. But if we see ourselves in common cause with the Indigenous Peoples of Suriname, if our survival is bound up with their survival, then this work is not optional. It is exhausting and frustrating to live in a homeland under siege, as the Wayana do, along with Indigenous and vulnerable peoples across the globe. Indigenous Peoples under siege never get to take a break from oppression. So we also must not take a break when we feel exhausted or frustrated. Our mutual survival depends on our persistence in doing the work of resistance.

I appreciate the wall of moms as a story of true solidarity, not only because of the work this group of privileged women did to cross the line but also because of the important work that followed. Ultimately, the wall of moms coalition submitted to the leadership of women of color. In crossing the line, Bev Barnum and the leadership of the wall of moms embarked on a bumpy journey where they gained a deep education in the systems of oppression that continue to endanger African Americans in the United States. Ultimately, it was decided that this group needed to be led by the people who have the lived experience of oppression. Crossing the line does not mean you get to be the hero in the story. It simply means that you have awakened to the reality of oppression that is intolerable, and you have aligned yourself with those who do not live in that condition by choice. It always means giving up power. As long as the dominant culture benefits from the oppression of the vulnerable, aligning one's self with the oppressed will have a cost—the cost of losing the power to oppress, whether actively or passively.

Call to the church: Cross the line

The prophet Isaiah writes:

> The LORD arises to accuse;
>   he stands to judge the peoples.
> The LORD will enter into judgment
>   with the elders and princes of his people:
> You yourselves have devoured the vineyard;
>   the goods stolen from the poor are in your houses.

How dare you crush my people
   and grind the faces of the poor?
   says the LORD God of heavenly forces. (3:13-15)

There are many reasons not to respond to this call to do right—to cross the line—in order to seek justice and defend the oppressed. Here are a few that I hear frequently:

- Things are worse somewhere else. There is suffering everywhere that is overwhelming.

- The solutions are not within my direct sphere of influence.

- We need to change our hearts and communities first.

- Our institutions are entangled financially.

- We need to protect our jobs.

- We need to protect our retirement.

- I need to find work-home balance.

- There is not much I can (personally) do.

- We can support "good stewardship" with biblical texts, too.

As I described in chapter 3, when I brought Indigenous concerns to the World Council of Churches Assembly, a respected international leader told me: "We can't be sidelined by one 'issue'—we need to focus on peace." This was his response when I asked the coalition of historic peace churches at the WCC to advocate for dismantling the Doctrine of Discovery at the international level.

I responded to him that we as Indigenous Peoples are not an issue, but a People with a message of hope for humanity—a humanity without hope.

Many churches are engaged in initiatives of symbolic solidarity, some of it expensive and exhausting. This is good work. However, the call I am lifting up is for Christian institutions to cross the line. It is time to sacrifice your financial security as long as your financial security is what endangers the powerless. I am lifting up a call to resist! To say no!

This call is not for divestment. Divestment is passive. Rather, I am asking the church to use the resources gained by investments in extraction to fund the resistance of the communities most harmed by extractive industry. What I am describing is something more than shareholder accountability, which often takes the form of letters sent to boards of directors, following a process set up by the extractive company that allows for reflection but not redress. What I am calling for requires deeper commitment—using your wealth to leverage support for those oppressed by extraction.

Here are some ideas. If you own stocks invested in extractive industry, give those most impacted the ownership of the share and, therefore, the power to determine what ought to happen with that stock. This action actually balances power. Another way of sharing power would be to give the entire increase in the valuation of the stock to those most impacted. In other words, if you are invested in an extractive industry and that stock makes you $20,000 over five years, you "owe" the impacted communities that money. You will still own the stock and thus retain interest in the corporation along with the access this provides, while choosing not to benefit financially from it. This transfer of wealth/assets (different from money alone) means joining in the position of the powerless—facing the consequences of extractive industry's behavior. If you know your stock portfolio will shrink if you can't benefit from stock in extractive industry, then invest yourself in reforming the corporations that are endangering Indigenous and vulnerable peoples. In either option—giving the oppressed total ownership of the stock or funding resistance to structural evil with the income from the stock—your wealth is diminished.

Investors with institutional power and moral authority, like church institutions, can also demand direct negotiation for human rights between companies and impacted communities. This is what I mean: a church institution can simply confront a mining company and invite the company into direct negotiations with the communities hurt by mining. This action is true peacemaking because it challenges structural violence perpetrated by the powerful. Peacemaking as it is commonly understood focuses on the vulnerable; specifically, we ask them not to defend themselves and their families using violence. When the vulnerable try to defend their homes, as the Miskitu people have done during ongoing land grabbing (see chapter 7), their self-defense is described as "aggressive," and "destabilizing."

If we wait on the institutions to change (the United Nations, the World Bank, the Organization of American States), we will never succeed. Their policies have been created to benefit the powerful. Rather, Christian institutions must struggle for direct negotiation between the powerful and the powerless, placing themselves in the position of the powerless. It is in our best interest to seek justice if we refuse to benefit financially until justice is served.

Using our power

I have heard from many quarters that it is better to try to effect change from inside oppressive institutions. As investors. As professionals. As people with power. A longtime friend from my home congregation told me, "Sarah, how will you help anyone if you impoverish yourself? It's better to have the money you need to do good work. If you put yourself at a disadvantage, you are defeating your own purposes!"

Many people of faith have told me over the years, "Take care of yourself first." This is often a response to my family's choice to not participate in the stock market by forgoing retirement accounts. But I cannot be burdened by a dual allegiance. If I choose to financially benefit from the oppression of my people, then I find I have two interests: one interest is protecting my own comfort and security, the other is advocating for my people. Which will ultimately win in the internal struggle between two masters?

The Wayana have just one allegiance, and that is to their survival. So, too, that must be mine. Their survival and my survival are one. If I am "hurt" by my nonparticipation in economic systems, then it is in my best interest to advocate for just systems. By nonparticipation in the stock market, I cross the line and align myself with the Wayana. By making myself vulnerable, I am motivated to resist. It is no longer a theoretical or symbolic exercise: I am on the hook, as they are.

That said, I acknowledge that I have privilege as a North American that goes beyond simple wealth. I have access, by virtue of my citizenship in the most powerful nation on earth, to advocate directly to institutions. I speak English fluently. I am well-educated. I understand the culture of the West and the culture of capitalism. I am a Christian.

These are all assets I can mobilize to resist the systems of oppression that threaten my people, Indigenous and vulnerable peoples everywhere. These assets, when joined together with hundreds or thousands of communities of faith, are enough to reshape reality. When I think about the communities of faith rising up, I am reminded of this text from Philippians:

> Therefore, if there is any encouragement in Christ, any comfort in love, any sharing in the Spirit, any sympathy, complete my joy by thinking the same way, having the same love, being united, and agreeing with each other. Don't do anything for selfish purposes, but with humility think of others as better than yourselves. Instead of each person watching out for their own good, watch out for what is better for others. (Philippians 2:1-4)

This text articulates the dream of a church united for justice.

Restorative justice and repair

In 2017, the United Methodist Women asked if I would help identify a path to reparations for Indigenous Peoples. Together, a working group and I envisioned a process where a trust would be established that would reserve a percentage of funds earned by the sale or lease of land, buildings, and all property in the United States. These funds would be returned to Indigenous Peoples of the United States as redress in repair for the damage done by the Doctrine of Discovery, knowingly or unknowingly, and to the advantage of the denomination. Since land had been stolen, income generated by land would be returned. A percentage of the trust would be designated for land return; monies could otherwise be used by Indigenous individuals and groups to meet the minimum standards of survival, dignity, and well-being identified in the United Nations Declaration on the Rights of Indigenous Peoples. The trust would accrue income for 233 years—the duration that the denomination had been in place in the United States and benefiting from lands Indigenous Peoples had lost.

The above vision for reparations was never adopted by the denomination. They weren't ready for it. However, it started a vital conversation in the United Methodist Church that spread to multiple denominations. What would redress look like? How could any institution afford it?

Since 2017 my thinking has changed, in part because I think financial reparations alone do not equate to true repair. While the funds collected for property sales would no doubt provide much-needed resources to those who have suffered at the hands of structural evil, it would still amount to charity. It would not balance power. Balancing power requires that the powerful reduce their power by handing a portion of it over to the vulnerable, the historically excluded. Right relationship requires giving up power. Sharing power means sharing a fate, so that we share the same risks, so your survival is bound up with mine.

Reparations, including the model I endorsed in 2017, have traditionally been conceived as transactional. Those who have benefited from injustice are sanctioned or else willingly choose to pay a penalty for past harms committed. In a transactional approach, the beneficiaries of injustice, in this case the beneficiaries of the Doctrine of Discovery, do not share risk with those brutalized by the systems of death. While the beneficiaries may experience discomfort because of a financial "hit," their well-being or security is not at risk. They do not risk the same fate with the oppressed. Once they have "paid their debt," they are free to move on.

You don't want sacrifices.
    If I gave an entirely burned offering,

you wouldn't be pleased.
A broken spirit is my sacrifice, God.
You won't despise a heart, God, that is broken and
crushed. (Psalm 51:16-17)

This text from the Psalms is about repairing harm. This
entails identifying the harm that has been done and repairing
the harm, the relationship with the victim, and the relationship with God. There is also acknowledgment that there will
not be peace or security on the land or among the people until
this occurs.

Restorative justice changes the frame from a punishment
paradigm to a focus on identifying harm done, and then repairing that harm. In a punishment framework, the locus of action
is judging guilt and meting out consequences. In a restorative
framework, the locus of action is repairing relationship. In this
frame, the purpose of repair is conciliation, or establishing and
repairing relationship where harm has been incurred. Many
Indigenous People I have known reject the idea of "reconciliation" with the Christian church because true relationship has
not been attempted. There can be no reconciliation without
first having conciliation.

Holistic reparation, or repair rooted in restorative justice, is
rooted in relationship. The goal is to build ongoing and long-
term entanglement. There is no "moving on" from the perspective of restoration, because a relationship has been created.

True repair means shared risk—entanglement. Mutuality.
Partnership. Taking up common cause. There is no formula
for how to achieve it. But I think it means collaborating with
Indigenous Peoples to find out.

NINE

My Cosmology

I MET GILBERT, A SARAMAKA tribal member, in Suriname. As we worked closely with tribal communities asking for our help to diagnose their own community health, it became clear that we needed a common language. Our basic assumptions about the world were simply not the same. For example, as we brainstormed intervention strategies together, one community suggested that we collaborate with the mining company polluting their food and water, a strategy that had simply not occurred to us.

Dan suggested that we use cognitive mapping, a qualitative interviewing technique designed to help uncover mental models or basic assumptions about the world. Rather than ask specific questions, cognitive mapping asks an individual to list all the elements about a topic and then put them into a spatial map, arranging the topics in a way that makes sense to them. Gilbert agreed to be the first tribal member to be interviewed.

We asked Gilbert to describe "mining" in his community. He seemed genuinely stumped, unable to generate any words that he felt related to mining. After about a half hour, we concluded that maybe Gilbert lacked substantive experience about the mining process, or its impacts. Next, we asked him to list elements related to "community health." Again, he seemed unwilling to list any elements related to community health. He seemed genuinely frustrated.

Although Gilbert spoke English, we asked him to come to a second interview, where we would work with a translator so that he could speak in his own language. In the second interview, Gilbert seemed again unable to generate any elements related to the topics we proposed, although we struggled with the translator to explain the process in multiple ways. "I want to help," Gilbert said, "but I don't understand what you are asking." In fact, Gilbert seemed unable to speak from an individual perspective at all, with himself as the reference. The translator explained that whatever we asked, he said he felt he couldn't respond. "He doesn't think he is the right person," the translator told us. "He keeps saying, 'You have to ask the others.'"

Finally Dan asked, "If this isn't working, what do you think might work?"

"If you give me a camera, I could take pictures, then explain them to you," he said.

We gave him a camera, he took pictures, then gave us the film to develop so that he could create a cognitive map using images.

What we found most surprising was what he chose to take pictures of. Almost all of them were images of the natural world. As he arranged his photos in relation to each other, explaining his map, he told us about the sacred places in his community—what had taken place at these sites and what they signified to his people. He told story after story—some from generations past, others more recent. He never spoke from his own point of view, but carefully discussed what he shared with us from the perspective of the group. At the very end he related his detailed explanation to "mining" and "community health," describing the impact of mining on the very heart of his people, which is embedded both physically and spiritually in the land of his people.

Dan and I were being schooled in Gilbert's cosmology—his fundamental understanding of the world—and his cosmology was not made up of discrete elements that could be written on a card. His community was embedded in the natural world, where the spirit world, the past, the present coalesced into a demonstrable reality. "We will stay here for all time," he said, "among the bones of our people." He paused, staring at us intently. "If we leave, it will only be in a box."

While we had asked Gilbert to explain something in a clinical, linear way, showing clear cause and effect, Gilbert was not able to unwind the elements of his reality from each other. We were asking him to describe an "objective" reality through the lens of time (cause and effect), while his fundamental understanding of the world was related to space (land). The land provided the lens of reality: everything life-giving came from it, and threats to it threatened the very existence of his people.

The theologian Vine Deloria Jr. explains this dissonance in "cosmology," or fundamental worldview, in this way:

> American Indians hold their lands—places—as having the highest possible meaning, and all their statements are made with this reference place in mind. Immigrants review the

movement of their ancestors across the continent as a steady progression of basically good events and experiences, thereby placing history—time—in the best possible light. When one group is concerned with the philosophical problem of space and the other with the philosophical problem of time, then the statements of either group do not make much sense when transferred from one context to the other without proper consideration of what is taking place.[1]

I tell this story to illustrate the fundamental differences between the cosmologies of the dominant culture and Indigenous Peoples. In what follows, I will attempt to explain different concepts and practices of spirituality, but I want to start by communicating this to you: for Indigenous Peoples, all of reality, including an understanding of God, is rooted in land.

This has been my experience when I've been invited to particular Indigenous places of worship. In the Washit Long House I have been honored to visit, ceremony is oriented around space, not time. In the Shaker Church, community members leave cell phones and watches by the door; how one enters the room has significance, as does how one exits. Ceremony is understood in the dimension of space. This is also true in the hogan, as well as when making offerings outdoors. The centrality of space is not simply a matter of ritual—it is indicative of a fundamental understanding of reality, and an essential understanding of God.

Reverence versus faith

Wrestling with the Doctrine of Discovery—and the Christian church's role in dismantling it—for nearly a decade has pulled me into relationship with Indigenous elders from across the globe. Many of these men and women are heroes to their own people; they are activists and leaders, thinkers and theologians. Conversation with them has helped me to glimpse existence from an Indigenous cosmology and provided me a perspective about the nature of reality, which really begins with insight on the nature of the Creator.

Romans 1 states:

> This is because what is known about God should be plain to them because God made it plain to them. Ever since the creation of the world, God's invisible qualities—God's eternal power and divine nature—have been clearly seen, because they are understood through the things God has made. So humans are without excuse. (vv. 19-20)

This Scripture is consistent with an Indigenous worldview—that the nature of the Creator is evident in the creation. What does creation tell us about God's divine nature?

Indigenous Peoples have been accused of animism—that is, worshiping the creation rather than the Creator. But really, the basis of Indigenous spirituality is reverence. The Diné (Navajo), my relatives from New Mexico and Arizona, "do not worship the Sun, or the sun bearer, as supposed," Steve Darden, my Diné mentor, instructed me. Rather, they express reverence for the Spirit of Life, the Creator, by finding elements of the Creator's nature in the Sun—faithful, unfailing. Giver of Light. Giver of life.

What else can we infer about the nature of the Creator?

Faithfulness. In the environment where I live, in the foothills of Pahto, the sacred mountain of the region, I see the faithfulness of the Creator with each season. In spite of the consistent inputs from agribusiness (herbicides and pesticides, nitrates and effluent); carbon emissions that are changing our climate; hydropower that pollutes, divides, and diminishes watersheds; in spite of our collective efforts, each spring, life returns to the soil, trees and plants flower, and pollinators do their important work to spread the miracle of life. We humans do nothing to earn this. We do not collectively give thanks. Yet each spring returns faithfully and, with it, life.

The interconnectedness and interdependence of the entire cosmos. The Yakama practice reverence in their spring feast, giving thanks before they go to gather. The elders instruct us: take just what you need. Leave plenty for future generations. This implies that life is interdependent; what I do has a direct impact on the lives of other creatures.

Living in ways that are consistent with this basic understanding results in abundance. The land where I live is rich in diverse plants, including elderberry, chokecherry, and golden currant. I harvest berries from the canes of these plants to make juice and jelly. Behind the calving sheds, a stand of currant bushes flourishes, and is shared with flocks of doves and blackbirds. If I wanted to pick the maximum number of berries to produce the largest amount of juice possible, I could strip the plants of every single berry. We might have surplus juice the first year, but ultimately, this hoarding behavior would diminish the propagation of additional plants. However, by taking just what our family needs and leaving the lion's share of the fruit for the birds, we ensure the propagation of additional plants. As birds eat berries and fly throughout the land, their droppings seed additional plants. Through simple observation, we learn the areas that have the water and soils necessary for currants to flourish. By taking just what we need, we are cooperating with the processes of life, ensuring we will have more than enough.

We learn from creation the processes of life—the nature that is self-evident in the Spirit of Life—and our place in it.

I have been taught by Indigenous elders to value reverence. Reverence is the foundation of the spirituality I have been taught. Steve has spent many hours with me in prayer and ceremony, and taught me to call plant life that surrounds us the "standing green nation." We are dependent on them for food and shelter, holding soil and preventing erosion, cleansing carbon dioxide from the air, and providing oxygen. There are so many things this nation does for us, without petition or thanks. They feed and shelter us—a society themselves that provides for us, a society that we depend on.

My experience of spirituality in the dominant culture is to value faith. Faith, from my point of view, is believing in something that I cannot see or prove with my senses. Despite overwhelming doubt, I believe anyway.

Reverence is deep respect. The Creator is evident in creation, which surrounds me. I can see it and experience it with my senses. I am part of it. Humility is acknowledging that I am not separate from creation; I am part of a web of life. I have been taught that this mutual dependence is a gift. Life is a gift. "Faith," or belief in something I can't see, is meaningless in my experience of Indigenous cosmology.

Living on an organic ranch where we raise beef, I encounter people from time to time who criticize participation in growing and harvesting animals. I feel a deep sense of connection to the animals I am part of raising and, truthfully, raising animals has made me consider becoming a vegetarian. But I have learned that whether or not I eat animals, I cannot separate myself from the food web, because I cannot separate myself from creation.

Let me consider a thought experiment.

My family cultivates small numbers of animals on 120 acres of pasture seeded with a variety of native grasses, forbs, and shrubs we manage as an ecosystem. Cultivation of native plants means we can rely on groundwater and annual rain (although we get just five to seven inches per year), rather than irrigation. Our animals have free choice of food on five pastures. They are not penned or fed grain. This management system ensures that our ranch is habitat to dozens of species of birds, mammals, amphibians, reptiles, and insects.

If we were to convert our fields to corn, wheat, and soybeans, the primary crops consumed in a vegetarian diet, habitat for dozens of species of birds, mammals, amphibians, reptiles, and insects would vanish. The animals that make this land their home would die along with their habitat. Were we to raise soy, corn, or wheat, we would use more fossil fuels; we would use an additional twenty-five million gallons of irrigation water, taking vital moisture out of the aquifer; we would drain the wetland that acts as a natural filtration system and is home to traditional plants like wapato, toolie, and willow; we would effect the death of thousands of animals, further shrinking vital habitat that is already dwindling in response to large-scale agriculture.

I say this not to justify raising beef but to make the point that regardless of whether I choose to eat beef or soy, I am part of a food web that has an impact on animals. In order for my family to eat, plants and animals must be sacrificed. This is an acknowledgment that I am part of creation; I am not and cannot be separate from it. It is not subordinate to me. It is *me*; I am it. Recall the display at the Yakama Nation Cultural Center Museum that states *When the hunter climbs to track his prey, he knows his brother waits for him.* We are connected. The survival of one determines the survival of the other. The "prey" is not objectified, or subdued; his life is equal to any life; his sacrifice is honored.

Creation is ongoing. Creation did not occur in six days and then stop; it is an *ongoing* process. Reverence means demonstrating deep respect for the plants and animals required to sustain my life and the lives of my family members.

An elder and friend, Mark MacDonald, explained to me that the miracle Moses experienced when he spoke to God through a bush on fire was not that the bush burned without being consumed by flame, but rather that Moses was able to see its true nature. Look around you—all around us the Spirit of Life burns in creation. And again, on the road to Emmaus—the Spirit of Life burned within the disciples, the same Spirit that burns within us.

That Spirit is with us, burning, this very moment.

The nature of the Creator is clearly seen.

Mutual accountability. Reverence does not happen once per week; it is practiced each day faithfully, moment by moment. It is acknowledging that we are dependent on the systems of life, that they are not subordinate to us or to our will. Steve Darden taught me to give thanks every single morning for life itself. The Yakama people give thanks for water before every single meal. The first people of the land where I live give thanks for water habitually. Making reverence a habit.

The statement of the Indigenous caucus to the World Council of Churches 10th Assembly made plain these threats to life, especially from the extractive industry:

> The extraction of natural resources of all kinds, of minerals, natural gas, petroleum, timber, and hydro-power, among others: threatens the waters, air and land that are sacred to us and

mean life for all human beings and all of creatures; removes us from our traditional sacred lands where our spirituality is rooted, and threatens the food web that we and all living creatures are dependent upon; enables genocidal effects to human beings, where Indigenous Peoples, vulnerable peoples, and the poor are evicted, displaced, poisoned, and killed so that multi-national economic systems can reap benefit for a few beneficiaries.[2]

Interdependence implies that we have an impact on the world around us, that we actually influence the very process of creation. The WCC 10th Assembly Indigenous caucus authors articulate:

> We as Indigenous Peoples believe that the Creator is in Creation. God revealed himself/herself as Creator and Sustainer in the act of creation. The triune God along with land co-parents all life. The mystery in John chapter 1 unfolds how the Creator abides in creation. The incarnation of God in Christ becomes totality in God's creation. The Creator was and is in Creation, and thus incarnation of God in Jesus Christ is an integral part of God's self in creation. Through God all things were made, without God nothing was or is made. In God there is life, and in God is the light of all Creation. The presence of God made the world and therefore is sacred. The work of creation in God is the unity of diversity, where all lives coexist in a harmonious balance because they are all from God. Each seed that sprouts begins creation anew, and not one seed can grow unless the Creator enables it. We believe that doing justice to God's creation is the basis of liberation and the human search for selfhood.[3]

How do we work together with the processes of life?

As discussed in chapter 6, mission must focus on restoration for all of creation, including all people. A transversal worldview is an understanding that you are "all my relations."

Yet the focus of the Western Christian church has been on the individual, with a fixation on confessing one's own personal sins, often centered around individual sexuality. One's relationship with the Redeemer is private, and transformation is primarily imagined as the Redeemer's individual plan for one's own life; the joint work of the Redeemer and self is in perfecting one's behavior. This individually-focused conception of spirituality, at its best, is blind to structural violence, and at its worst absolves us of the obligation to participate in collective repentance and to confront and dismantle systemic injustice. The focus of Christian mission has been on saving individual souls (often equated to reforming individual sin) rather than on the restoration of life and the systems of life.

The transversal worldview, by contrast, acknowledges that systemic injustice is injurious to all of creation, because harm to one is harm to all.

As I have noted, in Suriname the tribal people practice Winti. The Winti are the spirits of natural elements and ancestors. As I mentioned previously, in Winti spirituality, hatred is taboo. It is believed that one can kill simply by hating. When a conflict emerges, a healing ritual may involve the entire family and an invocation of ancestors. It is believed that conflicts set in motion in past generations may have led to current conflicts.

While this may sound absurd to those in the dominant culture, in fact, hatred gone unchecked *does* lead to death. This is demonstrated in blood feuds around the globe that rage on as war through generations. From an Indigenous multigenerational worldview, where it is understood that reality has been shaped by those that have gone before us and that many current dynamics are the result of past events, I think the self-centric belief that each of us is creating our own separate reality is the worldview that sounds absurd. *Of course* past events lead to current consequences. Yet there aren't mechanisms in the dominant culture to deal with conflict on this level—to understand its origins and work across multiple generations to address it.

Despite this wisdom, and despite multigenerational analysis of peacemaking, Winti has been characterized as witchcraft by Christian missionaries. The message of hope offered by Winti practitioners is ignored or discarded. Because it does not focus on individual redemption, but rather focuses on collective restoration; because it does not focus on a linear story of a specific, historical redeemer, the good news of Winti is dismissed.

Right relationship means giving up power

Dan and I moved to the Yakama reservation in 2006, where we continue to stay. We were drawn to the homeland of the Confederated Bands and Tribes of the Yakama Nation to seek peace in this place, what Mennonites call "right relationship," where power is balanced between people. I honestly believed then that I could behave in a way that would lead to right relationship. In the years since, I have learned that I was wrong, and to think I could singly balance power was simplistic and naive. In a context where the wealth of a people is wrongfully taken, and even the means of survival that remain are dominated and controlled, it is impossible to balance power between individual people. For right relationship to be possible, the structures that enforce inequity must be dismantled.

As you now know, Dan and I work as colleagues with Indigenous Peoples in South and Central America who are living with the impacts of resource extraction. We felt drawn to making a home in an Indigenous context here in the United States. I am an Indigenous woman myself, a Mennonite woman, married to a white man, mother to a son who can easily pass as white. I grew up in a city, far away from my own People, because both of my parents were orphans who were themselves assimilated as children. I had a lot to learn about the reality for many Indigenous People in the United States, and moving to a reservation provided quick instruction.

I met Vanessa (Van) when she and her three younger brothers stopped by soon after we moved into their neighborhood. Our closest neighbors, the family lived in a small home that included Van, four of her younger siblings, her mother, and grandmother. During that first visit, the children marveled at the inside of our twelve-hundred-square-foot modified mobile home, exclaiming, "You have a refrigerator!" and "You have doors on your kitchen cabinets!" and "This is the biggest house I've ever seen!" They made frequent stops at our home after that. They played in our yard, and we shared produce from our garden, including fresh eggs. Operating an organic ranch, we shared beef at the end of each month when food was low at Van's house. We also provided rides from time to time when a child missed the bus or when gas money was low.

When Van turned fourteen a few years after our son was born, I offered her a summer job, and for eight weeks or so she came by a few times a week to hang around the kitchen, helping with canning and baking, working in our large garden, and playing with my son. She saw how cash was collected from beef sales when we arrived home from farmers' markets on weekends, and how we kept what we'd earned in a small cash box, destined for deposit on Monday mornings.

One Monday, as Dan went to deposit the cash sales we had collected over the weekend, he discovered that an entire weekend of sales—a large sum—was missing from the cash box. We immediately went to Van's home and asked her about it. She admitted she had taken the money and spent it almost instantly. This was more than a small loss for us. Van's mother and grandmother were angry at Van and embarrassed by what she had done. Since the entire family lived on one small paycheck, it would be impossible for the family to repay what Van had taken. We explained that our trust had been violated and that reestablishing trust would be difficult, but that we would honor our relationship with the family and we would not press charges against Van.

The next summer, we tried again. Van came by each day, helping me with chores in the kitchen or the garden. She especially enjoyed helping with the dozens of chickens we hatched and raised that year. During one visit, Van raided the cash box, this time taking a few hundred dollars. Again, we went to her grandmother and mother, explaining the loss and confronting the young girl. Again, she admitted what she had done with many tears. Again, the money was already spent, and there would be no way to pay it back.

I felt crushed. We had developed a relationship with this family, sharing the produce from our garden and farm. We were there when members of the family died, helping with food, compassion, childcare. I felt we had done everything right. How could this child violate our trust in this way? I felt utterly betrayed. Didn't this family understand that we were doing the right thing by choosing to live in their community?

In the midst of this internal turmoil, I would come to understand this essential thing—my family is the beneficiary of a system of laws and policies that were created to crush a sovereign people. We could not be the "good guys" in this story. The farm where we live was once the original allotment belonging to Van's family. The land has been bought and sold many times since, land that cannot be owned in the cosmology of its original people. For how can land be owned? It is the same as claiming to own the wind. Creation is a force so powerful that Indigenous leaders in what is now Washington State were incredulous when Governor Stevens offered to buy it in 1855.

What is held sacred by the laws of the United States is private property—not creation or even human lives. If we wished to pursue our rights as property owners, we could have had Van incarcerated. We could have jailed the most vulnerable person in this story—a child living in poverty, surrounded by an empire designed to destroy her people. It was when my anger was focused on this child that the irony of the situation was made obvious to me. I, an Indigenous woman, a pacifist committing my life to human rights, felt angry enough to consider calling the police to protect my rights by incarcerating a child who did not own a refrigerator. Looking back, I am thankful that this insanity was made obvious to me at last.

Even if Van burned our house to the ground, she couldn't really hurt us—our home insurance would insulate us from financial harm. How could I possibly balance power with some produce or a summer job? This family understood very well what we could not at first see. We had already won the right to take everything away—land, privacy, self-determination, dignity, hope. They watched us each day as we *drove* our one child to private school, to piano lessons, to karate. Their family only intermittently had a working vehicle, and walking or hitchhiking was the norm, whether in hundred-degree heat in the summer or freezing temperatures in the winter. They saw the abundance of clothes and toys our son had—ten times more than they shared altogether. Their birthright, the land we felt entitled to, produced food for our family that we could *choose* to share, or not—it belonged to us. Among the Yakama, an item need only be admired to be presented as a gift, as generosity is prized above possessions. In the Yakama cosmology, a reasonable person shouldn't have to *ask*.

We cannot be the victims in this story. We have only one role—colonist. Beneficiaries of an unjust system. I realized finally that *the system must be dismantled*. No act of charity could right the massive inequity that is lived each day by the original Peoples of the land who lost everything when the reservation system was created. I understand differently now the story of independence in South Africa, where Black Africans were finally allowed to vote when the apartheid system fell. But decades later, South Africa remains one of the most violent countries on earth. Eighty-five percent of the land (food, diamonds, gold, water resources: for all of these things are land) is still owned and controlled by a tiny white minority. How can *freedom* be truly felt without *land*?

The Yakama lost much of their land—their access to food, shelter, spirituality, family life, culture, even their economy—when Governor Stevens created the reservation, and the Allotment Act took even the reservation land away just thirty years later. With the damming of Celilo Falls on the Columbia River (the source of "clean energy" in Washington State), the heart of the Yakama economy was cut out and replaced with nothing. No access to food. No access to trade or money. No access to transportation. All the wealth taken away. These things are not my personal fault.

But they are to my personal benefit if my family has the power and wealth to possess land stolen from the Yakama.

I finally realized that I will be able to engage in right relationship—relationship where power is balanced—when the laws and policies that created this unjust reservation system are dismantled. In order for power to be balanced, I must give up power, and convince others to do the same.

My family and I continue to be in relationship with Van's family. We share moments of pain, loss, death, and also celebration and birth. I realize that my work is not the work of Van or her family, and it is certainly not their job to validate me. I long for future days when my son's children may begin to form relationships built on a foundation of justice. Until then, I will work to fight laws and policies that prevent us from forming human relationships where the dignity of each of us is acknowledged in reality, in the air we breathe . . . in the law.

Reparations and private property

In the spring of 2020, I was privileged to participate in a private listening session where family members of missing and murdered Indigenous women in my community were able to speak with federal authorities about their experiences. The first speaker began by describing the destruction of Celilo Falls. What does a dam have to do with murder? I could see the question in the eyes of the authorities listening as she spoke. Celilo Falls was the center of economic, social, and spiritual life for the Yakama people for untold generations, and it was lost with the damming of the Columbia River for hydropower in 1957.

The loss of Celilo Falls marks the irrevocable breakdown of essential systems, because economy, language/culture, kinship group, family unit, government, and spirituality are all tied to land. Loss of the land and forced removal from land, including the internment of children to boarding schools and federal urban relocation programs, meant the destruction of essential systems for Indigenous Peoples. The result is homelessness, domestic violence, addiction, and the symptoms of the complete breakdown of economic and social systems.

Like the Wayana in the rainforest of the Guiana Shield, the Yakama have historically depended on fish as their primary source of protein. There is a story here in my community that says in the early days of creation, when all beings could talk to one another, the Salmon People made a commitment to always provide for humans. Each year, Salmon swim upstream against a mighty current to keep that promise. Yet since the damming of Celilo Falls, most Yakama people are now cut off from this vital resource. The primary lifeway, fishing, was deeply diminished and nearly destroyed.

As the speaker at the listening session talked about the loss of her niece, who was brutally murdered, she related it directly to the loss of Celilo Falls. In fact, each speaker at the event tied the trauma of losing a murdered family member to the loss of culture, community, and land.

Remember that the Allotment Act of 1887 served to further deprive the Yakama people of their lands to the point that less than 13 percent of the people who inhabit the 1.4 million acres of the Yakama reservation are Native American, and only 90,000 acres (6.4 percent) are held in trust by the tribe.

Although it is my great privilege to live on this land that has been so coveted, it is not a matter of good luck. Nor is it easy to undo what is done.

Dan, Micah, and I live on 120 acres in the homeland of the Confederated Bands and Tribes of the Yakama Nation. I think about my home when I think about private property, and the Allotment Act particularly. What is ownership of 120 dry acres at the foot of Toppenish Ridge to a river people, dependent upon salmon for survival?

Traditionally, Yakama communities migrated on a circuit, from spring ground where there are roots to harvest in the foothills, to summer ground where there are huckleberries and game in the high places on Pahto, to the river and valley floor during fall, and winter camps protected from the wind. What would it mean in 1887 to have 120 acres that do not provide any of these essential foods or seasonal patterns? What would it mean to be expected to live alone, away from the collective— even to compete with one's family members and tribal members—in the production of corn or grain? It runs counter to what the people know about how to be human. That is why a woman speaking about her murdered niece sixty-three years after the damming of Celilo Falls still makes the connection. The loss of this vital center of economic, social, and spiritual life, this structural violence, has led to physical violence—to the murder of her relative.

Private property is an erosion of community and collective identity, survival strategies core and fundamental to humanity. Private property is divisive for all people. Private property disconnects us from each other and from responsibility for each other. This is true for all people groups, not just for the Yakama, not just for Indigenous Peoples.

Thinking ecologically

Thinking ecologically is fundamental to an Indigenous cosmology. While ecological thinking focuses on conservation practices, it also focuses on the mutual embeddedness of natural systems. It expands the lens from private property and individual action to the entire watershed or food web, and the necessity of working collectively.

In my family, conservation is something we think about constantly on 120 acres, where we conserve twenty-five million gallons of water each month during irrigation season. But believing one can conserve a portion of the water table in our valley is the same as trying to "conserve" four square inches of water in a full bathtub. What a neighbor puts in the water table (pesticides, herbicides) flows to the rest of the water table, or "bathtub"; what we take out in irrigation and wells is drained from the rest of the system. Fences are imaginary when it comes to water. This goes for soils, as well. Trying to conserve soil on 120 acres in the context of a 2.7-million-acre valley is like putting sunscreen on a dime-sized portion of your face, believing you can protect one patch of skin from cancer. Fences are absolutely imaginary when it comes to air. Although my family farm burns very little fossil fuel to operate our beef business each year, there is no way to "protect" the air our son breathes from the large corporate producers nearby who use heavy equipment and burn large amounts of fossil fuel.

In the context of this reality, private property benefits the powerful. Corporate dairies and concentrated animal feeding operations in my community use their private property "rights" to dump harmful waste products on the reservation, including large amounts of cow manure that deposits unsafe levels of nitrates in groundwater.[4] The public health impacts of these practices endanger a community without state protections, since reservations are not subject to state environmental protection laws, and federal regulators are slow to respond to contamination in our small rural community.[5]

The church and reparations

In the years since many amazing people and I formed the Dismantling the Doctrine of Discovery Coalition, I have spoken with Christian church leaders across multiple denominations. Every church body I have spoken with is superficially supportive of coming to the aid of Indigenous Peoples threatened by extractive industry enabled by historical laws and policies put in place by the Doctrine of Discovery. Each one voices support for reparations, superficially. But not one has made an institutional commitment to these things, beyond issuing statements.

In 2019, I was approached by Mennonite World Conference (MWC) to co-host a convention session on the MWC Declaration of Solidarity with Indigenous Peoples, a declaration that I had contributed to drafting. I agreed, although skeptically. In the work of the Dismantling the Doctrine of Discovery Coalition, we had approached the MWC to help reach out to a colonist community in Mexico that is experiencing conflict with Indigenous Peoples; Indigenous Peoples living in the area had asked the coalition for help. We were rebuffed, however, and told that the MWC would not intervene in a global situation unless it directly pertained to a member congregation.

However, when the MWC sent a delegation to meet with an Indigenous member congregation in Panama that is struggling to have legally established titles to their ancestral land recognized and enforced, it was a similar story. Though the Panamanian community asked the MWC for advocacy in international forums such as the United Nations and the government of Panama, to my knowledge, little substantial action has been taken on their behalf.

This story is a common one in the global church.[6] There is rarely substantial connection with non-Christian communities struggling for justice. Even on behalf of Christian communities, there is sympathy with little follow-through. There is no explicit acknowledgment of how the Christian church, especially the North American church, benefits financially from extractive industry.

Church bodies are invested in extractive industry just like other institutions. Financial holdings, including retirement funds, are invested in gas, oil, and mining. And advocating for the vulnerable Peoples harmed, displaced, and killed by processes of extraction, it is believed, will threaten financial security for pastors, teachers, administrators, and missions.

But investment in systems that destroy the health and well-being of Indigenous Peoples destroys health and well-being for all of us. Extractive industry causes destruction and death for every ecological system upon which human life depends. Extractive industry, and the products and systems this juggernaut enables, threatens every life support system on earth. Reparation in this context is more than sharing a small portion of an annual budget; it is a commitment to healing systems endangered by extraction. It is a commitment to giving up one's illusion of financial security in favor of rejecting systems that threaten systems of life. It means risking the loss of your own security to challenge systems of death that seek to destroy the vulnerable first, but will ultimately destroy us all.

Many Indigenous Peoples in North America believed that land could not be owned; we are part of the land, the land is part of us. "We are the land," my son told me on our morning walk together, "we aren't separate from it." When Christians behave as though we can own creation, we are degrading all ecosystems that support life. This includes water, soils, air, and animals. Is a skin cell separate from its body? Believing we are separate from creation is a commitment to systems of death. When soils fail, when the air is unsafe to breathe, when our watersheds are contaminated, these signs indicate that death for people will soon follow. Every community of life, whether insect, animal, or human, understands this on some level. How can large groups of us forget this? Is our short-term "security" enough to deceive us into thinking we can somehow make ourselves safe in a world whose life-support systems are failing?

As a church, do we stand where we say we do? Many of us believe that we and our institutions stand with the oppressed. In reality, the church as a body collectively benefits from harming the most vulnerable people. Engaging in repair will mean turning away from this violence by risking our own security to challenge the powers that threaten us all.

The legacy we will leave to our descendants will be life.

Reimagining the good news

I was privileged to meet Mayra Gomez Perez, sister to my beloved Maria Chavez, the Bolivian leader I discussed in chapter 3 who inducted me into the work of dismantling the Doctrine of Discovery. After Maria's death, Mayra explained her own cosmology to me this way: "Earth is my body, water is my blood, air is my breath, fire is my spirit." The spirit of the Creator is in the earth itself. As Stan McKay taught me, centered in creation. God present to us in the fabric of creation obligates us to concern ourselves with the well-being of all creation, and all the systems that sustain life. Mission, solidarity, and action must all focus on redemption for all of creation.

The transversal worldview, and understanding that we are all relations, obligates us as a church to move beyond our obsession with individualism and personal piety, to collective repentance and seeking justice. We are collectively accountable for structural injustice and collectively obligated to work to restore justice for the oppressed and the systems that sustain life on the earth.

The transversal worldview also obligates us to accept the good news offered by Indigenous spirituality. That means seeking good news beyond the worldview of Christianity. What is the good news offered by Indigenous Peoples that is consistent with Jesus' mandate? What is the good news offered to us by Indigenous spirituality that is redemptive for the Christian church? Indigenous cosmologies instruct us that God is with us: God's eternal power and divine nature are manifest in creation.

It is time for us to move beyond ideologies that bring violence, injustice, and death. It is time for us to shed individualistic ideologies that seek to *negate* Jesus' mandate to bring good news to the poor, liberty to the captives, freedom for the oppressed.

Moving forward requires us to seek right relations with Indigenous Peoples. That means balancing power. Balancing power requires us to give up power. Give up the assumption that we hold the exclusive truth. Give up the claim that we have the right to dictate the terms of morality. Give up the privilege of assets that result in death. Give up the assumption that we "own" land assets, and that we should preside over how they should be "wisely" distributed. Moving forward requires relationship, repentance, and conciliation in mutual relationship.

According to the model of restorative justice, when harm occurs we must first acknowledge and understand the harm from the point of view of those wronged. We must then seek repair. Voicing apology and requesting forgiveness happens when resolution is in sight. It is not the first step, but near the last.

We are far from being in the position to voice apology. But I call on the church to acknowledge wrongdoing and begin the process of seeking repair in relationships with Indigenous Peoples.

TEN

People of Faith, Rise Up!

co-authored with Sheri Hostetler

AS YOU HAVE been on this journey with me through this book, perhaps you, too, have been stirred by the elder Dina's prophetic call: "Help us! Help us or go away." Perhaps you, too, have been asking the question Dan and I have been asking for sixteen years: "But what can I do to help?"

This chapter is about what you can do. Let me rephrase that: This chapter is about what *we* can do. I want to be very clear that dismantling the Doctrine of Discovery is not something that one person does.

The dominant culture in our country is highly individualistic. We have been socialized to see problems as individual ones, and so our interventions are often individualistic: recycling, buying an electric car, giving money to famine relief, providing money so an Indigenous child in Suriname can attend a boarding school in the city. When faced with a social issue, our first inclination is often to ask, "What can I do? What individual action can I take to help?"

While it is often important to take these individual-level actions—they do relieve some suffering—our most vexing social issues are not going to be solved by individual actions. I hope by now that is clear! Although I know each one of us reading this book tries to be a good person, the truth is, we are ensnared in sinful global systems that cause great suffering, suffering that is completely hidden to most of us most of the time.

This is structural sin. Not the sin of an individual—the sin of a system. And it is by far the most prevalent sin in which we participate. It is by far the sin that produces the most suffering in the world. It is not the sin of intentional or willful cruelty. Most people are not intentionally or willfully cruel; we may all feel sorrow when we hear of a child developing a neurological disorder because she consumes fish from a river polluted with mercury. Neither is structural sin the kind of sin we can lay at the feet of particularly greedy or racist individuals—as if by removing them from power or converting them the suffering will go away.

Rather, structural sin is sin that inhabits our lives by virtue of the policies, practices, institutions, and assumptions that shape how we live. It is sin so baked into the system, so much a part of how things are, that it is largely hidden, unseen except by those suffering from it—and sometimes not even then, because of the power of the system to blind even those oppressed by it to the true cause of the suffering.

This book has been an attempt to help you see, to make plain what is hidden.

Fortunately, our Scripture sees structurally, and it can help hone our vision. The Hebrew prophets name and expose structural injustice clearly and consistently. Jesus, in the tradition of these prophets, names and exposes the "domination system" of his day, and proclaims an alternative kingdom based on "upside-down" power arrangements and nonviolent love for all of us enmeshed in these structures. Paul also names and exposes structural sin. He calls it "the powers and principalities" that exert control over our lives.

Once we see the structural nature of what we are dealing with, I believe we can then turn away from feelings of guilt, which I notice are often the first response people have when I start talking about my partners in Suriname. Guilt is an individualistic response to what is perceived as an individualistic problem: "I did something wrong, so I have to fix it." Once we realize that we are all involved in structures that are sinful, we can instead focus more productively on dismantling the structures that manufacture inequity. Indigenous Peoples around the world are still under attack, specifically by policies that favor resource extraction over human rights and human health. We need allies in dismantling the laws and policies that lead to oppression and death. Let's not allow guilt to stall and prevent us from accessing our mutual potential in genuine relationship.

So how can we begin to do this?

For congregations:
Join our coalition—or start one of your own

In 2014, I founded the Dismantling the Doctrine of Discovery Coalition with Mennonite pastors Anita Amstutz and Sheri Hostetler (who wrote this chapter with me). We knew that there were people within Mennonite and Anabaptist circles working on various aspects of Indigenous justice. We wanted to bring them together to lift up and magnify the work we were each doing and to begin to collectively build a movement to dismantle the Doctrine of Discovery and its ongoing ramifications.

We held our first coalition meeting in the fall of 2014 and have been meeting annually since then. In between annual meetings, our working groups engage with our constituents through regular newsletters and fundraising (60 percent of the monies raised go to Indigenous partners doing work to dismantle the Doctrine—we call these "repair partners"—and the rest goes to the coalition to fund our work); create educational materials and events related to the Doctrine of Discovery; and actively seek to dismantle the laws and policies that remove Indigenous People from their lands, culture, and self-determination.

Building on the good work that Mennonite Central Committee Central States had already done with its "Loss of Turtle Island" exercise,[1] a participatory learning experience, and other resources, the coalition has produced many educational materials (all available on our website dofdmenno.org):

- a documentary about the Doctrine of Discovery, with an accompanying Bible study and resource guide

- a traveling exhibit

- in partnership with Ted & Company, a play about the Doctrine of Discovery (*We Own This Now*)

- a study guide on reparations

- a board game (in development) that will help players learn historical concepts and identify aspects of current-day injustice tied to the Doctrine of Discovery

- a podcast, *Dismantling the Doctrine of Discovery*

All of these educational efforts have borne fruit. When we began the coalition in 2014, not many Mennonites we came across at meetings and conventions had heard of the Doctrine of Discovery. Today, it is mentioned frequently in Mennonite spaces.

Our efforts to dismantle laws and policies have been equally as varied. We have taken the following actions:

- Organized people of faith across the United States to support the Miskitu people of Nicaragua, at the request of Miskitu elders in exile. Delegations traveled to Washington, D.C., educating lawmakers about the connection between economic development and the suppression of human rights for the Miskitu. The Nicaragua Human Rights and Anticorruption Act of 2018 was the result, wherein dollars issued to Nicaragua by the U.S. government for economic development grants are tied to human rights standards.

- Organized people of faith across the United States to uphold the Indian Child Welfare Act (ICWA), a key piece of civil rights legislation aimed at keeping Indigenous children housed and cared for with their parents, extended relatives, and communities. This legislation has been under attack for decades, but was struck down in federal court in October 2018. We were contacted by the National Indian Child Welfare Association to mobilize people of faith to advocate for the ICWA. In August 2019, the law was upheld in the Ninth Circuit Court of Appeals. We are still working with congregations to raise support for this crucial law in Texas and Indiana, states that filed with the defendants for the removal of the ICWA.

- Supported the ongoing efforts for self-determination in the Guiana Shield, where Dan and I continue to work alongside Indigenous Peoples advocating for environmental protection from mine waste.

- Backed the San Carlos Apache efforts to save their sacred lands of Chi'chil Bildagoteel (Oak Flat) near Phoenix, Arizona, from a proposed copper mine.

- Provided ongoing support for Mayan communities who have asked for our help in navigating genetically modified organism pollution in Mexico's Yucatan Peninsula, as well as economic development programs that displace and endanger their communities.

We invite you to join us in this work! Please visit our website (dofdmenno.org) to find out ways to get involved. We lift up this coalition and its activities as just one model that people of faith from different traditions could draw from as they seek to collectively dismantle the Doctrine of Discovery.

Many other denominations have also begun this work, and some have issued statements repudiating the Doctrine of Discovery. If you are interested in getting involved alongside your own faith tradition or denomination, a good way is to find out what your church is already doing. Although you may not be aware of it, your denomination may already be engaged in this work! The next step is to find out how you can get involved to take the next steps within your congregation.

For church institutions: Participate in direct peacemaking

When I speak of church institutions, I am referring to denominations (like Mennonite Church USA and the United

Methodist Church) and all the different organizations connected to them—financial institutions (that, say, provide retirement investing); educational institutions (like high schools, colleges, and universities); relief and development agencies; organizations focused on social justice, service, and evangelism; and so on. Really, I am referring to any body that has a sphere of influence within a denominational or religious tradition.

We as peacemakers following in the way of Jesus can be involved in *direct* peacemaking. What do I mean by that? I mean that these institutions can band together and, for instance, ask corporations dumping mercury into rivers in Suriname to enter into direct negotiations with the communities affected by this pollution.

What if a coalition of church-related colleges banded together to ask the church financial institution that manages their retirement funds to put pressure on mining companies in which they are invested to hold direct negotiations with communities harmed by the mining? This is what I call direct peacemaking. It is my experience that we will not get redress for adversely affected communities if we try to intervene with the international structures that wield power. For example, in Suriname, we have not been able to get redress for impacted communities by petitioning the Inter-American Development Bank, the international human rights mechanisms, or the government of Suriname itself. But interventions with extractive industries in direct negotiation with communities have been successful.

This strategy has worked before. A mine in Suriname was releasing cyanide into the watershed. Animals and plants were dying every time this cyanide was released, and of course people were also being poisoned. The nonprofit organization I founded with Dan—Suriname Indigenous Health Fund (sihfund.org)—

purchased cyanide test kits and distributed them among affected communities so they could collect their own data on cyanide emissions in their waterways. As soon as the mine found
out that communities were measuring the amount of cyanide
discharged into their watersheds, they immediately wanted to
engage in negotiations with these communities. Community
leaders also invited the government of that district to be a part
of these talks. Together, the affected communities, the mining company, and the government figured out a solution that
worked for all of them—in this case, a clean source of drinking
water that wasn't going to be harmed by the cyanide dumping.[2]
The corporation provided rigs to drill for non-contaminated
water, and the government provided solar power. It was easier
for the mining company to do this than to deal with lawsuits
stemming from cyanide poisoning or with aggrieved communities engaging in direct actions like blockading the entrance to
the mine or damaging the mine in some way.

You may notice that I am not calling on either individuals
or institutions to divest from extractive industries like mining. When you sell your stock in Newmont Corporation, for
example, someone else just buys that stock. This change in
who owns the stock does nothing to help communities on
the ground who are experiencing pollution from Newmont's
mines. Instead, we should call corporations to account. We
should tell them the impact their corporate practices are having on people, and we should ask them to be in direct contact with the communities affected. An intermediary group
will likely need to be a part of these negotiations, and many
denominations have relief and development agencies that
work in or near communities threatened by extraction. These
agencies could serve as intermediaries in such negotiations, as

could the local NGOs with whom these agencies often partner. In some instances, SIHF or our coalition could serve as an intermediary organization. You could also find out more about what your denomination's relief and development agencies are already doing within Indigenous communities. Agency workers on the ground may be working with local Indigenous communities who are seeking relief from and redress for pollution related to mining or other extractive industries. Ask them how you can come alongside their work for justice.

If the corporations refuse to enter into these negotiations, we could start a campaign among people of faith to put pressure on them until they do. We could ask people to lobby Congress, to write letters to the editor, to take all sorts of creative actions[3] to convince the corporations that it is in their interest to directly negotiate with affected communities, just as the mining company dumping cyanide in Suriname found it in their interest to negotiate after we gave communities kits to test cyanide levels.

What if we asked our denominational mission boards to fund missionaries to corporations, to minister to people and companies bound by the powers and principalities and to invite them to liberating practices? What if those missionaries were funded to do the sort of work I am describing here?

The truth is, many churches are sending missionaries and aid workers to countries where communities are harmed by unjust corporate practices. They bind the wounds of those harmed but often do so without calling out the injustice that wounded them in the first place. And in some instances, the people who are doing the work are aware of the injustices and are trying to be heard by the denominations, but people in the churches would rather fund a well or a hospital. When people are forced off their land because of the legacy of the Doctrine of Discovery and suffer impoverishment and negative health impacts as a result, churches (and other NGOs) often step up to meet the healthcare and housing and food needs of these people. All the while, the corporations that generate wealth from this dispossession are not being asked to pay the cost of the harm caused. In economic terms, corporations have externalized the cost of doing business to churches.

Why shouldn't corporations be held responsible? Why can't churches collaborate to hold them accountable—to ask that their costs of doing business actually reflect the costs of doing business? This isn't what happens right now, and the supranational structures I talked about in chapter 7 have, so far, ensured that this is the case. This would all be more effective than divestment.

But let me also be clear: If you are making money from investments in extractive industry, it is unjust to keep that money. You must turn around and invest that money in the communities being harmed by extractive industries like gold mining, oil and gas drilling, and so on. (Please see chapter 8 for more about this.) That—and engaging in direct peacemaking—is the only way to justly stay invested in those industries.

The fact is, churches have a lot of power. Dan and I have approached Columbus Gold to ask them to negotiate directly with communities impacted by the mining in French Guiana. But frankly, Columbus Gold does not care what two people like us have to say. However, if church bodies that remain invested in Columbus banded together to petition them, change might happen. If those same church bodies used the dividends from those investments to fund activists who are trying to gain self-determination for communities impacted by extraction, change might happen. If those same church bodies used those dividends to fund missionaries to corporations involved in extraction, change might happen.

The church has been part of ending unjust structures before! Apartheid was a system of massive injustice that had tentacles beyond the nation of South Africa itself. South Africa is one of the richest countries on earth in terms of natural resources. Many people and corporations in the Western world were getting rich off those natural resources. The World Council of Churches originally intervened in this oppressive system by funding organizations resisting apartheid in South Africa. They did this through the Programme to Combat Racism. Eventually, they participated in an international campaign for sanctions against South Africa that ultimately helped dismantle apartheid.

Sometimes, people tell me that they can't get involved in ending unjust corporate practices in Suriname because they don't know any Indigenous People there. To my mind, this would be like someone saying they couldn't get involved in the struggle against apartheid, because they didn't know any Black South Africans. Apartheid was an unjust structure, and you didn't need to know anybody directly impacted by it to advocate for its ending. The same is true for structures related to the Doctrine of Discovery.

For church institutions: Change the structures

Over the sixteen years we have been trying to seek redress for our partners in Suriname, Dan and I have come to the conclusion that the implementation of just a few interventions would change the world—for all of us:

1. *Change the paradigm that regulates corporations.* In the United States, corporations must seek the financial interests

of their shareholders above all other interests, including the public good. Canadian law professor Joel Bakan exposed the impact of this paradigm in his 2004 book *The Corporation*, which was made into an award-winning documentary that same year. Bakan claims that corporations are designed to behave like sociopaths, or "externalizing machines," that maximize profits by keeping wages low while externalizing real social, environmental, and economic costs that must be borne by society.[4] While there is some public debate about whether corporations are legally obligated to maximize shareholder wealth, the corporate paradigm certainly operates as though this were true.[5] If we simply changed the language in the law, placing the public good above or even equal to the financial interests of shareholders, we would change the world.[6] No longer could corporations legally poison people or the planet.

2. Litigate environmental and human rights violations by U.S. corporations in U.S. courts. Corporate actions that pollute the environment and violate international human rights standards are often completely legal. This is because national laws in developing countries where resources are extracted are often framed or reformed to make investment in extraction activities attractive to investors. When communities are injured by mining or other extractive industries, they do not have legal redress in their own countries, because the laws have been formed to support extractive industry. For example, if the environment has been polluted, there may be no redress, because regulations have been formed to ensure pollution is not penalized.

International human rights conventions, the international structures that transcend national laws, are weak. This is because international organizations that frame human rights conventions are charged with honoring the sovereignty of member states. In most cases, human rights conventions are entered into voluntarily by individual countries, which often means the conventions are essentially nonbinding. In the context of corporations headquartered in the United States, if U.S. corporations were obligated to follow their own national environmental and labor laws for their activities overseas, they could be sued by injured community members in U.S. courts. It would be expensive for them to pollute the environment or exploit workers, and the incentive to take advantage of poor regulation of human and environmental health abroad would be removed.

3. Call for the enforcement of international policy that protects vulnerable peoples. Several global conventions have been created to bring a social contract to the international arena. These policies balance interests—whether government, local, social, or economic—and balance power by forcing discourse through a court of law. These conventions transcend both civil laws, within which individuals and communities can petition their own governments, and international treaties, which typically serve economic interests between nations. These conventions are negotiated in the sphere typically reserved for international treaties. They tacitly acknowledge the problems created by international arrangements devoid of a social contract, where individuals and communities have no ability to petition international structures or foreign entities like corporations or banks. Within my own country, I am enfranchised, which means I can seek redress if I find myself injured by a national party or policy. In the international arena, I have no ability to seek redress from a foreign entity if I find myself injured by it. Conventions articulate a solution to this problem by identifying a forum within which parties are able to voice their interests and negotiate resolution. Unfortunately, international conventions are not implemented. There is no enfranchisement for communities or individuals who find themselves at the mercy of foreign entities who have the power to remove their livelihoods, pollute their lands, and endanger their health or very lives.

There are several international conventions designed to protect the most vulnerable, including the World Health Organization's Health in All Policies. HiAP was established to acknowledge that all policy created, including economic policy, must include safeguards for the protection of human health. If implemented, this policy would ensure that health interests are included in all international policy.

In one of its resolutions, the United Nations Security Council has a principle, the "responsibility to protect," that if enforced would prevent systemic harm to Indigenous and vulnerable communities.[7]

The Inter-American Development Bank created the policy Development with Identity, which eschews forced assimilation in economic development projects. Unfortunately, forced assimilation has been the standard procedure in colonization. If this policy standard were enforced, the people affected by economic development would have the same rights and access as people in the developed world who benefit from a social contract. Here is an example of the social contract I enjoy. In the United States, if my property is taken away because of a government policy, according to the principle of eminent domain I have the right to be adequately compensated for my loss. So if a restaurant I own is demolished because it lies in the path of a railroad line, I stand to be justly compensated for my loss. If implemented, Development with Identity would create mechanisms for enfranchisement for all Peoples impacted by economic development.

The United Nations Declaration on the Rights of Indigenous Peoples (UNDRIP) was written by global Indigenous leaders and defines fundamental protections for Indigenous Peoples. Sadly, adherence to these policies is voluntary by individual countries. It has not been ratified by the U.S. Senate and therefore is not binding on the United States. Canada introduced a bill to adopt the UNDRIP in late 2020.[8]

We have the influence to insist that these policies be implemented. We can do this by referring to them as we negotiate direct peacemaking. We can abide by them within our own institutions, and can call on others to do the same.

Here's an idea: If the United States adopted these conventions, policies, and resolutions into our national law, it would change the world, because these policies would be enforceable within the borders of the most powerful country on earth.

Undertaking national legislation is neither simple nor linear. At first it can seem impossible—where do we start?! Yet the Democratic Party in the state of California adopted a resolution to make dismantling the Doctrine of Discovery a plank in its party platform in 2020.[9] This action was undertaken when a woman named Una learned about the Doctrine of Discovery at her church and was moved to take action. As a delegate of the party, she felt she could get involved and call for structural change. I was privileged to accompany her in this historic action as she built coalition within her party and got the votes to make this happen! This is a first step in potentially recruiting a legislative champion to get a bill to Congress.

This is not the only pathway for getting legislation adopted, but it serves as an amazing example of how the Spirit can move us when we listen. Our Dismantling the Doctrine of Discovery Coalition was able to participate in legislation that built human rights language into a law, the Nicaragua Human Rights and Anticorruption Act of 2018. We learned a lot as we did this work! We were all volunteers. None felt "qualified." Yet somehow, during a time of partisanship and gridlock in Congress, this law was passed.

The church has often been the vanguard of economic development; we must now choose to be a vanguard of justice and insist that these policies be implemented. We must call for a social contract, and stand our ground until the vulnerable are enfranchised.

I know that at this point there may be a desire for simple answers. Join with this group in the work they are doing. Give money here. Vote for that bill. Honestly, what I am suggesting does not yet exist. It has to be imagined first, then built together. This is how change happens. Daring to listen to the Spirit of Life; daring to imagine a world that is just. We know what needs to happen. It's going to take all of us: our collective gifts, our collective will, we the body, animated by the Great Animator. This is our job—to create a moral framework we call the world to follow.

We could do this! Churches in the United States, working in relationship with our siblings worldwide, have the power to influence and change our national laws. Canadians, Europeans, and people from countries around the globe can do the same. We can put justice above profit for the safety of vulnerable people everywhere.

We must all work together to call our church institutions— those whose identity is to follow the way of Jesus—to stand with us in this struggle. We can imagine together how we might make this a reality. Until individuals representing committed institutions stand together in effective ways with Indigenous and vulnerable Peoples, our words and gestures are merely hollow and symbolic.

Then there was a great protest of the people

In the book of Nehemiah, the Hebrew people have returned from exile in Babylon. They have finally escaped the grip of foreign oppression. But now there is another problem: the oppression is coming from within. A shortage of food has led to large-scale debt slavery[10]—people are literally selling their sons and daughters for food, as well as putting up their land and possessions as collateral so they can acquire money to pay taxes.

> Then there was a great protest of the people and their wives against their fellow Jews. Some said, "With our sons and daughters we are many, and we all need grain to eat and stay alive."
>
> Others said, "We have to mortgage our fields, our vineyards, and our houses in order to get grain during the famine."
>
> Still others said, "We have had to borrow money against our fields and vineyards in order to pay the king's tax."
>
> "We are of the same flesh and blood as our kin, and our children are the same as theirs. Yet we are just about to force our sons and daughters into slavery, and some of our daughters are already slaves! There is nothing we can do since our fields and vineyards now belong to others." (Nehemiah 5:1-5)

What a clear-eyed and deeply disturbing "seeing" of the problem. Those oppressed by unjust systems have come together, have accurately named the source of their suffering, and are collectively raising their voices.

Nehemiah, the governor of Judah, hears their outcry and responds with his own clear-eyed analysis:

> I was very angry when I heard their protest and these complaints. After thinking it over, I brought charges against the officials and the officers. I told them, "You are all taking interest from your own people!" I also called for a large assembly in order to deal with them. "To the best of our ability," I said to them, "we have bought back our Jewish kin who had been sold to other nations. But now you are selling your own kin, who must then be bought back by us!" At this they were silent, unable to offer a response.
>
> So I continued, "What you are doing isn't good! Why don't you walk in the fear of our God? This will prevent the taunts of the nations that are our enemies! I myself, along with my family and my servants, am lending them money and grain. But let's stop charging this interest! Give it back to them, right now. Return their fields, their vineyards, their olive orchards, and their houses. And give back the interest on money, grain, wine, and oil that you are charging them." (Nehemiah 5:6-11)

Everything the elites are doing in this passage was legally within bounds. While taking interest on loans was against Mosaic Law, taking pledges was permissible.[11] However, the whole point of not taking interest on loans was to prevent the rich from exploiting the poor. "Taking pledges" has resulted in the same thing. But the moneylenders are hiding behind the "letter of the law." Nehemiah wants nothing to do with this moral trickery. He tells them in clear terms what they are doing: You are enslaving your own kin, he says, and it isn't good.

Nehemiah then calls them to repentance. This repentance is not about feeling guilty and saying that they are sorry for their exploitation. Another step is necessary: restitution of what was taken.

> They replied, "We'll return everything, and we won't charge anything else. We'll do what you've asked."
> So I called the priests and made them swear to do what they had promised. I also shook out the fold of my robe, saying, "So may God shake out everyone from their house and property if they don't keep this promise. So may they be shaken out and emptied!"
> The whole assembly said, "Amen," and praised the LORD. And the people did as they had promised. (Nehemiah 5:12-13)

Change is possible! Gandhi's freedom movement in India released a whole country from colonial rule. The Southern freedom movement in the United States challenged decades of harsh discrimination against African Americans. Apartheid ended because of a vigorous social movement, as did the abolition of slavery. Systemic change has happened, and it can happen. These pernicious, evil, sinful structures which are bigger than we are as individuals have nevertheless been created by us together, and we collectively can undo them. While structural sin transcends individual moral agency, it does not transcend collective agency: The people can do as they had promised.

Let us always remember that our God is a God of justice. We are not alone in our desire and movement toward a more just way of living. As Cynthia Moe-Lobeda says, "The sacred life-giving and life-saving Source of the cosmos is always luring creation toward God's intent that all may have life and have it abundantly."[12] Martin Luther King Jr. said it this way: "Though the moral arc of the moral universe is long, it bends toward justice." The God revealed in Scripture—through the Hebrew prophets, through Jesus—is a God who is struggling with us and within us to bring about God's shalom.

Alone, each of us is fleeting: just one life that is easy to snuff out. But together we are stronger than the systems of death. What is true cannot be diminished by silencing one voice. Our thirst for justice is an assertion of the dignity that is ours. Our dignity cannot be given to us by the principalities and powers; it is our birthright and ours to have forever. Rulers may deny it or acknowledge it—but our dignity is not theirs to take away.

Our work is not easy, but it is profoundly necessary. The survival of life on earth depends on our ability to see past the reality designed to diminish us and justify the systems of death. The bonds essential to this reality cage us all with the logic of greed, selfishness, and determinism: the logic of death. We must find the courage to seek, create, and invent a reality consistent with the logic of life. Do not live in fear. Walk in certainty, in the nobility of a mighty spirit which you share with all creation. It is your right, your birthright, to seek out others to work toward a world you imagine, a world where we are all free.

Resources for Further Reading

Deloria, Vine, Jr. *God Is Red: A Native View of Religion.*
Fulcrum Publishing, 1994.

Frichner, Tonya Gonnella. "The Preliminary Study on the
Doctrine of Discovery." *Pace Environmental Law Review* 28
(2010): 339.

Jacob, Michelle M. *Yakama Rising: Indigenous Cultural
Revitalization, Activism, and Healing.* University of Arizona
Press, 2013.

LaDuke, Winona. *Voices from White Earth: Gaa-
Waabaabiganikaag.* E. F. Schumacher Society, 2005.

McKay, Stanley. "Speaking My Truth." In *From Truth to
Reconciliation: Transforming the Legacy of Residential Schools*,
ed. Marlene Brant Castellano, Linda Archibald, and Mike

DeGagné. Ottawa: Aboriginal Healing Foundation, 2008, 99–113.

Napoleon, Harold. *Yuuyaraq: The Way of the Human Being.* University of Alaska, Fairbanks, 1996.

Woelk, Cheryl, and Heinrichs, Steve, eds. *Yours, Mine, Ours: Unravelling the Doctrine of Discovery.* Intotemak, Mennonite Church Canada, 2016.

Notes

Contributor's Preface

1 Cynthia D. Moe-Lobeda, *Resisting Structural Evil: Love as Ecological-Economic Vocation* (Minneapolis: Fortress Press, 2013), 5. This book would be an excellent companion read to this book. It is not surprising to me that Sarah and Cynthia are friends!

Introduction

1 Roxanne Daniel, "Since You Asked: What Data Exists about Native American People in the Criminal Justice System?," Prison Policy Initiative, April 22, 2020, https://www.prisonpolicy.org/blog/2020/04/22/native/.

2 Sally C. Curtin and Margaret Warner, "Suicide Rates for Females and Males by Race/Ethnicity: United States: 1999 and 2014," National Center for Health Statistics, April 22, 2016, https://www.cdc.gov/nchs/data/hestat/suicide/rates_1999_2014.htm.

3 "The Condition of Education," National Center for Education Statistics, last modified May 2020, https://nces.ed.gov/programs/coe/indicator_coi.asp. See under "Public High School Graduation Rates."

4 "Poverty Facts: The Population of Poverty USA," Poverty USA, accessed January 22, 2021, https://www.povertyusa.org/facts.

5 "Peristats: Infant Mortality Rates by Race: United States, 2015–2017 Average," March Of Dimes, accessed January 22, 2021, https://www.marchofdimes.org/peristats/.

Chapter 1

1 While the City of Yakima chooses the spelling that uses *i* as the second vowel, the *Yakama* Nation chooses the traditional spelling used in the 1855 treaty, where *a* is the second vowel. The tribal council voted to adopt this spelling in 1994. See "'Yakamas' Alter Spelling of Tribe," *Seattle Times*, January 26, 1994.

2 Marieke Heemskerk, Katia Delvoye, Dirk Noordam, and Pieter Teunissen, *Wayana Baseline Study: A Sustainable Livelihoods Perspective on the Wayana Indigenous Peoples Living in and around Puleowime (Apetina), Palumeu, and Kawemhakan (Anapaike) in Southeast Suriname* (Paramaribo: Amazon Conservation Team Suriname, 2007).

3 Vanessa E. Grotti, "Christian Bodies, Other Bodies: Processes of Conversion and Transformation in Northeastern Amazonia," in *Native Christians: Modes and Effects of Christianity among Indigenous Peoples of the Americas*, ed. Aparecida Vilaça and Robin Wright (New York: Routledge, 2016).

4 "The Bull *Romanus Pontifex* (Nicholas V), January 8, 1455," Native Web, last modified March 23, 2012, http://www.nativeweb.org/pages/legal/indig-romanus-pontifex.html.

5 One could argue that the ideological framework of racism preceded the legal and theological justification (i.e., the Doctrine of Discovery), rather than vice versa. In other words, religious leaders believed that Christianity was the epitome of civilization, and thus anyone who wasn't a Christian was less than human. As a sociologist, I tend to believe that structures create ideas or ideologies more than the reverse. No matter what you think about which came first, however, the Doctrine of Discovery as a structure *and* as an ideological framework of domination is still the result.

6 A more detailed examination of policy eras that removed Indigenous Peoples from their lands, including their urbanization, is explored in chapter 4.

7 This is based on private correspondence with Inter-American Development Bank officials in 2005, and mining executives in 2019.

Chapter 2

1 One feature of the treaty not stressed with the tribes was that until the treaties were ratified by the U.S. Senate in Washington, D.C., whites were free to settle on reservation land. The Native Americans understood from Stevens that the treaties protected their lands. The whites understood from Stevens that the lands were open for settlement. In the June 21, 1855, issue of *The Oregonian* (Portland) in which Stevens announced the treaties (even though they still had to be ratified by the Senate), there appeared an announcement that gold had been discovered

in the Colville region of the upper Columbia. Prospectors began to flood into the Northwest across the passes and up the Columbia River to get to the new diggings. This put them across Yakama lands, where they victimized Native Americans and some Native American women—one the disabled daughter of Chief Teias—on the way. See David Wilma, "Yakama Tribesmen Slay Indian Subagent Andrew J. Bolon near Toppenish Creek on September 23, 1855," History Link, March 20, 2007, https://historylink.org/File/8118.

2 John Braun, "Liberating Children and Youth: A Biblical-Theological Study for the Use in the Local Church" (PhD diss., San Francisco Theological Seminary, 1980).

3 Delos Sacket Otis, *The Dawes Act and the Allotment of Indian Lands*, The Civilization of the American Indian Series 123 (Norman: University of Oklahoma Press, 2014), 9. First published 1973.

4 Otis, editor's introduction (1973 ed.), x.

5 Steve Newcomb, "The 1887 Dawes Act: The U.S. Theft of 90 Million Acres of Indian Land," *Indian Country Today*, February 8, 2012.

6 Harvard Project on American Indian Economic Development, *Yakama Nation Land Enterprise* (Cambridge, MA: Harvard Kennedy School of Government, 2008), 1.

7 Michelle M. Jacob, *Yakama Rising: Indigenous Cultural Revitalization, Activism, and Healing* (Tucson: University of Arizona Press, 2013).

8 Exec. Order No. 11,670 (Providing for the return of certain lands to the Yakima Indian Reservation), 37 Fed. Reg. 10431 (May 23, 1972). Text available at the American Presidency Project, https://www.presidency.ucsb.edu/documents/executive-order-11670-providing-for-the-return-certain-lands-the-yakima-indian-reservation.

9 Walt Crowley and David Wilma, "Federal Judge George Boldt Issues Historic Ruling Affirming Native American Treaty Fishing Rights on February 12, 1974," History Link, February 23, 2003, https://www.historylink.org/File/5282.

10 Lora Shinn, "As the DOE Abandons a Toxic Mess Threatening Columbia River, Yakama Nation Fights Back," NRDC, September 18, 2019, https://www.nrdc.org/stories/doe-abandons-toxic-mess-threatening-columbia-river-yakama-nation-fights-back.

11 The Environmental Protection Agency estimates that the average American produces 4.4 pounds of garbage per day.

12 I am a descendant of the Tewa people, from my home state of New Mexico. Living on the healing land of the Yakama, and living in community with the People of this land, has encouraged me to explore both the Yakama cosmology as well as the cosmology of my own people, the Tewa people.

Chapter 3

1   WCC Executive Committee, "Statement on the Doctrine of Discovery and Its Enduring Impact on Indigenous Peoples," World Council of Churches, February 17, 2012, https://www.oikoumene.org/resources/documents/statement-on-the-doctrine-of-discovery-and-its-enduring-impact-on-indigenous-peoples.

2   "Statement on the Doctrine."

3   "Statement on the Doctrine."

4   As I heard spoken by Mark MacDonald.

Chapter 4

1   Robert J. Miller, *Native America, Discovered and Conquered: Thomas Jefferson, Lewis and Clark, and Manifest Destiny* (Westport, CT: Greenwood Publishing Group, 2006).

2   Trade and Intercourse Acts of 1790, 1793, 1796, 1799, and 1802.

3   Removal Act of 1830.

4   General Allotment Act of 1887.

5   Quoted in Delos Sacket Otis, *The Dawes Act and the Allotment of Indian Lands,* The Civilization of the American Indian Series 123 (Norman: University of Oklahoma Press, 2014), 10–11.

6   Civilization Fund Act of 1819.

7   James Smith, *Away from Their Barbarous Influences: The Yakama Boarding School at Fort Simcoe* (Toppenish, WA: Yakama Nation Museum, n.d.).

8   Smith.

9   H.C.R. 108, 83rd Cong. (1953); State Jurisdiction over Offenses Committed by or against Indians in the Indian Country, Pub. L. No. 83-280, 18 U.S.C. § 1162 (1953).

10 *Federal Recognition: Politics and Legal Relationship between Governments, before the Comm. on Indian Affairs,* 112th Cong. (2012) (testimony of Bryan Newland, Senior Policy Advisor, Office of the Assistant Secretary for Indian Affairs). Text available at https://www.doi.gov/ocl/hearings/112/FederalTribalRecognition_071212.

11 Indian Relocation Act of 1956.

12 The Meriam report of 1928 reported the boarding schools were grossly negligent. However, there was not regular formal oversight, so information is inconsistent. Lewis Meriam, *The Problem of Indian Administration; Report of a Survey Made at the Request of Honorable Hubert Work, Secretary of the Interior, and Submitted to Him, February 21, 1928* (Baltimore: Johns Hopkins University Press, 1928), available at https://catalog.hathitrust.org/Record/009063777.

13 Genesis 25:18–33:20; Malachi 1:2-5; Romans 9:1-18.

14 Tonya Gonnella Frichner, "Preliminary Study of the Impact on

Indigenous Peoples of the International Legal Construct Known as the Doctrine of Discovery" E/C.19.2013/13, submitted to the Permanent Forum on Indigenous Issues, 9th session, New York, 2010.

15 Opinion provided to the court by Chief Justice John Marshall, *Johnson v. M'Intosh*, 21 U.S. 543, 572–73 (1821). Emphasis added.

16 *Johnson v. M'Intosh* at 573.

17 *Johnson v. M'Intosh* at 569–70.

Chapter 5

1 Stan McKay served as the thirty-fourth moderator of the United Church of Canada, the first Aboriginal person in Canada to lead a mainline protestant denomination.

2 Stan McKay, "Living in the Shadow of *Doctrine*," in *Yours, Mine, Ours: Unravelling the Doctrine of Discovery*, ed. Cheryl Woelk and Steve Heinrichs (Winnipeg: Mennonite Church Canada, 2016), 116.

3 William Galbraith Miller, *Lectures on the Philosophy of Law* (London: Charles Griffin, 1884), 404, quoted in Steven T. Newcomb, *Pagans in the Promised Land: Decoding the Doctrine of Christian Discovery* (Golden, CO: Fulcrum Publishing, 2008), 109.

4 Lewis Hanke, "The 'Requerimiento' and Its Interpreters," *Revista de historia de América* 1 (1938): 25–34, quoted in Newcomb, 35–36.

5 Harvey G. Neufeldt, "The Legacy of Jacob A. Loewen," *International Bulletin of Missionary Research* 32, no. 3 (2008): 141–148.

6 Jacob Abram Loewen, *Culture and Human Values: Christian Intervention in Anthropological Perspective: Selections from the Writings of Jacob A. Loewen* (Pasadena, William Carey Library, 1975), 386.

7 Loewen, 401–2. Emphasis in the original.

8 James Smith, *Away from Their Barbarous Influences: The Yakama Boarding School at Fort Simcoe* (Toppenish, WA: Yakama Nation Museum, n.d.), 1.

9 Kathy Tucker, "James H. Wilbur (1811–1887)," *Oregon Encyclopedia*, last modified January 23, 2020, https://www.oregonencyclopedia.org/articles/wilbur_james_h_1811_1887_/.

10 Tucker.

11 Vanessa E. Grotti, "Christian Bodies, Other Bodies: Processes of Conversion and Transformation in Northeastern Amazonia," in *Native Christians: Modes and Effects of Christianity among Indigenous Peoples of the Americas*, ed. Aparecida Vilaça and Robin Wright (New York: Routledge, 2016).

12 Marieke Heemskerk, Katia Delvoye, Dirk Noordam, and Pieter Teunissen, *Wayana Baseline Study: A Sustainable Livelihoods Perspective on the Wayana Indigenous Peoples Living in and around Puleowime*

(Apetina), Palumeu, and Kawemhakan (Anapaike) in Southeast Suriname (Paramaribo: Amazon Conservation Team Suriname, 2007), 6.

13 Grotti, 186.

14 Dan Peplow, "Indigenous Suicides—Individual Accounts of Collective Violence: A Highly Individual Crisis Caused by Social, Economic and Political Stressors," Suriname Indigenous Health Fund, May 2017.

15 Peplow.

16 Personal correspondence, May 9, 2019.

17 Richard Price, *First-Time: The Historical Vision of an Afro-American People* (Baltimore: Johns Hopkins University Press, 1983).

18 Henri J. M. Stephen, *Winti Culture: Mysteries, Voodoo and Realities of an Afro-Caribbean Religion in Suriname and the Netherlands* (Amsterdam: Karnak, 1998), 15.

19 Elisabeth Elliot, *The Savage My Kinsman* (New York: Harper, 1961), 123.

Chapter 6

1 Steven T. Newcomb, *Pagans in the Promised Land: Decoding the Doctrine of Christian Discovery* (Golden, CO: Fulcrum Publishing, 2008), 39.

2 Donald M. Scott, "The Religious Origins of Manifest Destiny," National Humanities Center, last modified September 15, 2016, http://nationalhumanitiescenter.org/tserve/nineteen/nkeyinfo/mandestiny.htm.

3 George E. Tinker, *American Indian Liberation: A Theology of Sovereignty* (Maryknoll, NY: Orbis Books, 2008).

4 Tinker, 138.

5 WCC Executive Committee, "Statement on the Doctrine of Discovery and Its Enduring Impact on Indigenous Peoples," World Council of Churches, February 17, 2012, https://www.oikoumene.org/resources/documents/statement-on-the-doctrine-of-discovery-and-its-enduring-impact-on-indigenous-peoples.

6 Robert Allen Warrior, "A Native American Perspective: Canaanites, Cowboys, and Indians," in *Voices from the Margin: Interpreting the Bible in the Third World*, ed. Rasiah S. Sugirtharajah (Maryknoll, NY: Orbis Books, 1991), 235–41.

7 Rev. Tore Johnsen served as the general secretary of the Sami Church Council from 2009 to 2016.

8 Tore Johnsen, "Listen to the Voice of Nature," in *God, Creation, and Climate Change: Spiritual and Ethical Perspectives*, ed. Karen L. Bloomquist (Minneapolis: Lutheran University Press, 2009), 101–13.

9 Ursula Länsman, "FolkWorld Scene from Inside: Sámi Culture and the *Yoik*," FolkWorld, last modified October 29, 2007, http://www.folkworld.de/9/e/sami.html.

10 Walter Sawatsky, *Going Global with God as Mennonites for the 21st Century* (Bethel, KS: Bethel College Press, 2017).

Chapter 7

1 A concession is a contract that gives a (usually) private company the right to operate a specific business within a government's jurisdiction. Concessions are often given to companies for the purpose of resource extraction, like mining of ores.

2 Marieke Heemskerk and Marilyn Olivaria, *Maroon Perceptions of Small-Scale Gold Mining Impacts, II: A Survey in Mining Camps and Affected Communities in Suriname and French Guiana* (Paramaribo: World Wildlife Fund–Guianas, Special Report, 2004).

3 Komyo Eto, "Minamata Disease," *Neuropathology* 20 (2000): 14–19.

4 While I have not witnessed major violence in Suriname, our work in Nicaragua with the Miskitu people demonstrates this point, as I will note later in this chapter. See "Nicaragua Is Promoting Illegal Land Grabs in Indigenous Territories—Report," *Guardian*, April 29, 2020, https://www.theguardian.com/world/2020/apr/29/nicaragua-illegal-land-grabs-indigenous-territories-report.

5 For a detailed analysis of the SLMP, see "Suriname," in *The Indigenous World 2007*, ed. Sille Stidsen (Copenhagen: International Work Group for Indigenous Affairs, 2007).

6 Ellen-Rose Kambel and Fergus MacKay, *The Rights of Indigenous Peoples and Maroons in Suriname*, IWGIA Document 96 (Copenhagen: IWGIA, 1999).

7 David Nathaniel Berger, ed., *The Indigenous World 2019* (Copenhagen: International Work Group for Indigenous Affairs, 2019), 213.

8 Kambel and MacKay, *Rights of Indigenous Peoples*, 145.

9 Kambel and MacKay, 84.

10 Kambel and MacKay, 140.

11 Kambel and MacKay.

12 Daniel Peplow and Sarah Augustine, "Intervention Mapping to Address Social and Economic Factors Impacting Indigenous People's Health in Suriname's Interior Region," *Globalization and Health* 13, no. 1 (2017): 11.

13 Berger, *Indigenous World 2019*, 216.

14 Daniel Peplow and Sarah Augustine, "Public Health Programs as Surrogates for Social Action in Suriname, South America," *Public Understanding of Science* 24, no. 1 (2015): 53–68.

15 Peplow and Augustine, "Public Health Programs."

16 Edward D. van Eer, Gustavo Bretas, and Hélène Hiwat, "Decreased Endemic Malaria in Suriname: Moving towards Elimination," *Malaria Journal* 17, no. 1 (2018): 1–9.

17 UN General Assembly, Resolution 61/295, UN Declaration on the Rights of Indigenous Peoples," A/61/L.67 and Add. 1 (September 13, 2007), https://www.un.org/esa/socdev/unpfii/documents/DRIPS_en.pdf.

18 I have described a few mechanisms we pursued seeking redress for Indigenous Peoples in the Guianas. We sought others as well. For a description, see our article that more fully describes attempted interventions with the Inter-American Development Bank as well as the U.S. Department of Justice, the International Committee of the Red Cross, and mining corporation responsibility: Daniel Peplow and Sarah Augustine, "The Submissive Relationship of Public Health to Government, Politics, and Economics: How Global Health Diplomacy and Engaged Followership Compromise Humanitarian Relief," *International Journal of Environmental Research and Public Health* 17, no. 4 (2020): 1420.

19 Cynthia Moe-Lobeda, *Resisting Structural Evil: Love as Ecological-Economic Vocation* (Minneapolis: Fortress Press, 2013).

20 Moe-Lobeda, 3.

21 John Paul Lederach, *The Poetic Unfolding of the Human Spirit* (Kalamazoo: Fetzer Institute, 2011), 6.

22 Moe-Lobeda, *Resisting Structural Evil*, 269.

Chapter 8

1 Tonya Mosley and Allison Hagan, "Wall of Moms' Organizer Calls on Fellow Suburban Mothers, People in Power to Fight for Black Lives," WBUR, July 23, 2020, https://www.wbur.org/hereandnow/2020/07/23/wall-of-moms-protests-portland.

2 Alan Paton, *Cry, the Beloved Country* (New York: Simon and Schuster, 2003), 208.

3 A shadow report is written by an NGO to highlight issues not raised by national governments (Universal Periodic Reviews are written by national governments). A shadow report can also point out where a national government may be misleading in its representation of the state of human rights in the country.

Chapter 9

1 Vine Deloria Jr., *God Is Red: A Native View of Religion* (Golden, CO: Fulcrum Publishing, 1994), 62–63.

2 "Indigenous Peoples Pre-Assembly Statement" (unpublished), World Council of Churches 10th Assembly, Busan, 2013.

3 "Indigenous Peoples Pre-Assembly Statement."

4 Letter to Washington State House of Representatives Committee on Energy and Commerce, November 8, 2017, by Helen Reddout, President Community Association for Restoration of the Environment, Inc; Chris

Wilke, Executive Director Puget Soundkeeper Alliance; Joshua Tsa-vatewa, President Friends of Toppenish Creek; Lauren Goldberg, Staff Attorney Columbia Riverkeeper; Lee First, North Sound Baykeeper RE Sources for Sustainable Communities; and Stephanie Hillman, North-west Campaign Representative Sierra Club. Retrieved from: https://docs.house.gov/meetings/IF/IF18/20171109/106603/HHRG-115-IF18-20171109-SD004.pdf

5 Jessica Owley, "Tribal Sovereignty over Water Quality," *Journal of Land Use and Environmental Law* (2004): 61–116.

6 By global church, I mean denominations and official church bodies connected to those denominations. There are inspirational faith-based NGOs that do this work, of course, such as Christian Peacemaker Teams. Imagine how much more effective they could be with the sup-port of denominations and their official church bodies.

Chapter 10

1 "The Loss of Turtle Island" is a participatory learning experience that depicts the historic relationship between European settlers—including Mennonites—and the Indigenous Nations, the original inhabitants, of the land we now call the United States of America. For more infor-mation, see "The Loss of Turtle Island," Dismantling the Doctrine of Discovery Coalition, December 6, 2018, https://dofdmenno.org/the-loss-of-turtle-island/.

2 I am aware that dumping cyanide into the environment is also not the fi-nal solution to this problem. However, one of the principles of our work is to prioritize the self-determination of Indigenous communities. It is up to them to determine the solutions that best meet their needs. This is another way that we, as the people with power, give up that power in order to let the communities themselves decide what they want.

3 See Gene Sharp's 198 different methods of nonviolent action in his book *The Politics of Nonviolent Action* (Westford, MA: Porter Sargent, 1973). I want to point out here that it is often necessary to change tactics according to the context; no one strategy is sure to be successful. Rather, working humbly in relationship and being flexible will enable us to respond creatively.

4 Joel Bakan, *The Corporation: The Pathological Pursuit of Profit and Power* (London: Hachette UK, 2012). First published 2004.

5 Cornell business professor Lynn Stout makes a powerful argument that this system of thought is not mandatory, although it is pervasive and damaging to the public good, corporations, and even shareholders. Lynn A. Stout, *The Shareholder Value Myth: How Putting Shareholders First Harms Investors, Corporations, and the Public* (San Francisco: Berrett-Koehler, 2012).

6 Leo E. Strine Jr., "Making It Easier for Directors to Do the Right Thing," *Harvard Business Law Review* 4 (2014): 235.

7 In paragraphs 138 and 139 of the 2005 World Summit Outcome document, heads of state and government affirmed their responsibility to protect their own populations from genocide, war crimes, ethnic cleansing, and crimes against humanity and accepted a collective responsibility to encourage and help each other uphold this commitment. They also declared their preparedness to take timely and decisive action, in accordance with the United Nations Charter and in cooperation with relevant regional organizations, when national authorities manifestly fail to protect their populations. See UN General Assembly, Resolution 60/1, 2005 World Summit Outcome, A/RES/60/1 (October 24, 2005), https://www.un.org/en/development/desa/population/migration/generalassembly/docs/globalcompact/A_RES_60_1.pdf.

8 An Act Respecting the United Nations Declaration on the Rights of Indigenous Peoples, Bill C-15, 43rd Parliament (2020). See https://parl.ca/DocumentViewer/en/43-2/bill/C-15/first-reading.

9 In the California Democratic Party section entitled "Equality of Rights and Opportunities," the language reads: "Denounce the Doctrine of Discovery as a violation of inherent human rights of individuals and peoples and support dismantling legal structures and policies based on that doctrine to allow Indigenous Peoples to self-govern." The action to support this language was undertaken by a congregation!

10 Wayne A. Meeks, *The HarperCollins Study Bible: New Revised Standard Version, with the Apocryphal/Deuterocanonical Books* (New York: HarperCollins, 1993), 722.

11 Meeks, 722.

12 Cynthia Moe-Lobeda, *Resisting Structural Evil: Love as Ecological-Economic Vocation* (Minneapolis: Fortress Press, 2013), 9.

Acknowledgments

FIRST, I MUST acknowledge my husband, best friend, and partner, Dan Peplow. The ideas expressed here are the product of years of shared labor, research, and conversation. While my name is on the cover, all my work is really the product of a collaboration between the two of us. There truly is no me without you.

I also wish to acknowledge Sheri Hostetler, without whom this book would not have been possible. As co-founder of the Anabaptist Dismantling the Doctrine of Discovery Coalition, Sheri has met with me nearly every week since 2014, and knows this material as well as I do. I am so thankful for her countless hours of labor in shaping and pruning every single draft. Her contributions and edits were invaluable, and she co-wrote chapter 10 with me. I want to thank Weldon Nisly, my pastor for many years, for believing in me and in this work, and for introducing me to Sheri.

Several readers contributed to the final stages of the drafting process. My mentor Steve Darden has provided healing, guidance, and support to me over many years, as well as sensitive input in the drafting of this book. Astrid Aveledo thoughtfully read and commented on drafts despite her numerous commitments, while she simultaneously engaged in important work as a community leader and executive director of a dispute resolution center. I am so thankful for Astrid's dedication, sensitivity, and commitment to speaking the truth as an Indigenous woman. Sabrina Porter Lindquist contributed hours of reading and writing in the form of detailed, wise comments that both challenged me to back up my assertions and to speak the truth. I want to acknowledge the partnership of editor Aimee Moiso from Herald Press; I am thankful for the grace she showed me in wrestling with difficult material further challenged by a cross-cultural conversation.

I must acknowledge the leadership and members of the Dismantling the Doctrine of Discovery Coalition for community, true solidarity, and partnership over many years. Anita Amstutz, Erica Littlewolf, Karin Kaufman Wall, Jonathan Neufeld, Katerina Friesen, Tim Nafziger, Luke Gasho, Carol Rose, John Stoesz, Alison Brookins, Ken Gingerich, Sarah Nahar, Jonathan Nahar, Jennifer Delantey, and many others have heavily influenced my thinking and writing. I owe each of you profound thanks.

I want to acknowledge that the dismantling journey occurred because of an invitation from Maria Chavez, Bolivian theologian and leader. Maria, the work continues. I also want to acknowledge the mentorship given to me by Tonya Gonnella Frichner, Onandaga woman and contributor to the United Nations Declaration on the Rights of Indigenous Peoples, who helped me navigate the United Nations system. The world is diminished by the absence of these fearless women.

I further want to acknowledge the Indigenous leaders, activists, and community members with whom it has been a privilege to partner in the Guiana Shield. Your bravery and endurance amaze me.

My thanks to friends and neighbors on the homeland of the Confederated Bands and Tribes of the Yakama Nation. It is a privilege to get to live here as a guest on your healing land.

I want to thank Cameron Altaras and Carol Penner for generously allowing me to include a revised version of the chapter I wrote for the forthcoming book *Resistance: Addressing Violence in a Peace Church.* I also want to thank Katerina Friesen for allowing me to include a passage I wrote for the forthcoming reparations resource for the Dismantling the Doctrine of Discovery Coalition.

Finally, thank you to Dan and Micah for helping with my chores, putting up with late nights, and allowing me the hours and hours over many months of sitting in my office, and our shared space, writing.

The Author

SARAH AUGUSTINE is cofounder and cochair of the Dismantling the Doctrine of Discovery Coalition and executive director of the Dispute Resolution Center of Yakima and Kittitas Counties. Augustine, who is a Pueblo (Tewa) descendant, has written for *Sojourners*, *The Mennonite*, *Anabaptist Witness*, *Response Magazine*, and other publications, as well as a variety of academic journals. She has consulted with the World Council of Churches, Methodist Women, the Episcopal Church, and other church bodies. She and her husband, Dan Peplow, and their son live in the Yakima Valley of Washington.